FRAN MACILVEY

HAPPINESS MATTERS

© FRAN MACILVEY 2017

The moral rights of the author have been asserted.
All rights reserved.

http://www.franmacilvey.com

Published by HEARTWELL PUBLISHING
© FRAN MACILVEY 2017

All rights reserved. No part of this publication may be reproduced, stored or transmitted in any form or by any means without the prior permission of the copyright holder except for brief quotations in critical reviews and other non-commercial uses permitted by copyright law. For permission requests please write to the publisher.

Cover design: Jane Dixon-Smith

ISBN: 978-1-9997136-0-7 (Paperback)
ISBN: 978-1-9997136-1-4 (Ebook)

CONTENTS

What Do I Know?	1
How Are You?	9
Do You Like Your Life?	15
Emotional Honesty	22
Get Out of Your Groove	27
Life is a Mirror	30
Cell Memory	40
Affirming What We Choose	45
Meditation and Visualization	51
I Am, Therefore I Choose	59
Power Chooses to Create	63
An Agreeable Life	68
Joy is Energy	73
Your Passions Fuel Your Joy	76
Taking Life ForGranted	86
Opportunity Knocks	95
Scripts and Subtexts	102
Asking For Help	107
I've Got My Own Keys	111

Hello Friend	117
Living in Black and White	124
Finding Light	129
Cause and Effect	133
Magnetism and Matter	135
Mind over Matter Makes our World	138
The Law of Reflection	142
What We Focus On Gets Bigger	146
What We Resist, Persists	153
Learning to Receive	158
Self-Sabotage	165
Surrendering our Attachment to Results	176
What Is Naive about Optimism?	184
Pessimism has its Place	190
Progress and Pain	202
To Have and to Hold?	206
We Are All Connected	214
Forgiveness	217
Living in the Present	230
Unconditional Love	236
The Journey Home	241
Notes	243
Appendix	245
Sources and Suggestions for Further Reading	246
About Fran Macilvey	249

I ACKNOWLEDGE THE LOVING SUPPORT OF

- My husband and my daughter, who have shown me what it means to live life to the full. Thank you for your faith in me.

- The Religious Society of Friends (Quakers) in Britain, membership of which is a continuous revelation.

- Lee Fitton, whose encouragement to write gave me the first objective assurance that I could.

DISCLAIMER

The author does not dispense medical advice or prescribe the use of any technique as a form of treatment for physical or medical problems without the advice of a physician, either directly or indirectly. The intention of the author is only to offer information of a general nature to help you in your quest for emotional or spiritual well-being. In the event that you use any of the information in this book for yourself, the author and publisher assume no responsibility for your actions.

None of the suggestions included in this book is intended to replace the care of a physician or to interfere with a diagnosis, prescribed medicines or therapies. Each suggestion is based solely around my own personal experiences and is never intended to substitute for existing care regimes.

"Without faith there is no vision; without hope our dreams die in a desert of sand; without courage we do not move forward; without patience there is no progress; without love there is no peace; and we cannot be happy within ourselves if we do not have each other."

By the author – in the style of
St Francis of Assisi's Prayer (see Appendix)

WHAT DO I KNOW?

My happiest memory, I used to say, was of a day at a beach, somewhere hot. A kind lady with a shock of glorious white hair and friendly, expressive eyes, held me up as we leapt in churning surf. I still recall the fierce pleasure, the mounting excitement and the thrill of being part of this most delightful game, active and buoyed up by a strong friend. She was a visitor, which made me all the more grateful for her company. I was about three years old.

I recall sitting on the kitchen step, singing my heart out for hours at a time. I was sending my voice out into the world to be active for me. Because I was born disabled with cerebral palsy, I did not walk until I was five-and-a-half years old and about to go to school. I passed hours sitting, watching others, inevitably comparing my awkward, shambling movements with the physical ease of those who played, ran and got on with their lives. Upon entering school I found it difficult not to sing in class, until I realised that I could be creative in other ways and was able to channel my energies into painting and colouring with crayons.

It was never going to be easy to answer the question, "Why me?" and I found it increasingly challenging to set aside my difficulties for long enough to enjoy what life had to offer. For decades, paralyzed by feelings of unfairness, I battled a maze of negative feelings: anger, depression, self-hatred and guilt. But one advantage of sitting for long periods is that I have had lots of time to ponder.

Only too aware of the mess that misery has made of my life, I have always yearned to find answers and to navigate through all the pain I have endured, to a life resembling happiness. Sorrow and frustration make me difficult to live with, physically ill and spiritually bereft. Yet even out of sorrow there may emerge a more enduring message, that we hold within us real power to choose personal change for the better. The more I discover, the more clearly shines the knowledge that, for physical, emotional and spiritual resilience, positive choices that bring happiness and personal peace are vital for a fulfilling life. There is nothing better for our prospects than laughter with our friends or the hope of a light at the end of the tunnel.

Changes in the way I perceive my reality unfolding continually refresh my understanding of what it means to be alive. The worn-out carpet of my older, dull patterns is gradually being replaced with a new tapestry of calming certainties in a dazzling vortex of brilliant colours. In the last few years, since I married a fine, loving man and we have been blessed with a beautiful child, I have become increasingly happy, though more often than I like to admit, the "old me" still pops up her head and does her best to try to spoil it all.

The responsibility for the care of our daughter, so often totally dependent on Eddie and me for learning daily lessons which would shape her whole life, drove me forward with my almost obsessive ponderings. (Over the years, my husband has become very used to being an audience of one at our "breakfast lecture" series!) One evening, as I was putting our daughter down to sleep, I experienced a dawning awareness that, in her natural state she was never cross or angry. I saw that, despite my frequent misjudgements and inept handling, she accepted sweetly what I gave and forgave all my mistakes. I determined to learn from her – and, first and foremost, to follow her example of release and forgiveness. I understood that she was teaching me, a most humbling awareness which was all the incentive I needed to keep going with my self-education.

There are so many lessons, which take so long to percolate that I am often tempted to quit. But here's the thing – I have always known that life is beautiful, a gift which can be filled with sunshine and laughter; and I feel unable to rest until I find a place that approximates to "peaceful", "understood", "loved" and "happy". We deserve to be happy and I have yearned to be, so nothing stops me looking, while any pain I uncover on the journey is simply something to accept, ignore or learn from.

Believing that life was something to be endured without being understood, for years I tolerated high and low mood swings, until in a new, braver frame of mind, endurance began to lose its appeal. I was on the lookout for any mechanism that drove this seesaw. What gave the swings such a push? Why did my moods change abruptly and so often? The answer that came was: guilt.

Before I lost this lead, which floated past as light as a ghost of a feather, I wrote out a list of all the things I have ever felt guilty about. It took a while, but when I felt I had them all down, I said, "Good, now that is all out in the open. I didn't feel much, as I was already deeply familiar with the "triggers" on my list, but I did return over the next few days, casually adding anything that I felt needed to be included. A process of exploration had begun, lighting a long fuse which fizzed while I slept.

I had a few dreams. One was of a pile of huge stone blocks piled up in a flat desert somewhere. In the bleak landscape, I could see clearly and with compelling simplicity, that when I smiled and let go, when I gave out lovingly, the blocks melted away into light. When I thought negatively and heavily about life, the blocks were right in front of me again, keeping out the light and blocking any way forward. Every day I was giving "obstacles" painful life and making them real and unyielding because of my insistence about them. The message was clear: holding on to judgment, criticism, guilt or any negative thought, blocks out understanding and forward progress. These blocks were barriers to deeper spiritual awareness. The only one trapped behind them was me.

It is not because *I owe* anyone anything, that forgiveness and letting go are so crucial: it becomes not a moral issue, but a practical and straightforward tool to help me achieve the best in life. Whenever I let go my attachment to a "bad" feeling or situation, immediately I experience a lighter reality, brimming with fresh possibility. Stumbling blocks vanish, the light of awareness can reach me and a path forward clears before my eyes. I was pleased and uplifted by the vividness of this understanding, which fitted snugly into everything else I was beginning to accept. And that was that, or so I thought.

Then I began to get ill and felt sore, paranoid and depressed. None of the many small, annoying kitchen cuts and scalds on my hands would heal. Believing I was probably overdue for another mood swing,

I hunkered down and waited. Guilt was suddenly everywhere in my thoughts; and I felt and appreciated its mammoth hold over me: it was smothering. An excerpt from the original list I compiled reads: "I feel guilty for not being good enough; for being lazy; for being complacent; for not working hard enough; for not knowing anything; for being and feeling awkward; for being an embarrassment; being in the way; letting the side down; being a disappointment; being stupid; being ungainly; being conspicuous; being different; being smug; being a waste of space; being flippant; having fun, being too honest, laughing, attention seeking…"

I was facing the crushing realization that guilt was so entrenched and all-encompassing in my life, I hardly noticed it. A thing can be so big we don't see it, exactly in the way that a large shady tree cuts out the daylight as it towers high over us, so high we forget it is there.

The point about unpicking the knots of unhappiness is, of course, that the threads of the fabric often go back far into the past. Of this I am well aware. But now I was beginning to understand the damaging effect that guilt has, when it is entirely caught up with everything we think and believe about ourselves. What caught me by surprise was the sudden realization that I felt guilty about absolutely everything. All my minor preparations had built up a tidal wave of awareness, overwhelming and finally liberating. During one long night, I saw how I had internalized guilt to a hideous degree, dragging it with me everywhere.

I finally faced a woman who chose abusive and unkind "friends", a woman who sought a punishing career, who gave away all her time, money, enthusiasm and strength on difficult or unrewarding relationships. Perhaps these examples are familiar enough to many of us. The point for me was that these examples are from a past which I *thought I had put behind me.* But consider also a woman who forgets to linger on what she enjoys because she should be "doing something else", who rarely laughs completely and who tries much too hard. I have even made a habit of searching out things to feel bad about, no matter how far in the past they may have receded. I seldom do frivolous, though sometimes that feels so delicious. I never order expensive. I have spent years even *sitting uncomfortably,* for goodness sake, because it "didn't matter" that sitting should be a comfort. That is not far from believing, "I don't deserve to be comfortable." It seems I have felt guilty – not good enough – just by living.

By believing in the reality and necessity of hardship, sorrow and loss, I have made my life un-necessarily difficult and painful. To a greater or lesser degree, we all do; and there is no reason to feel bad about the chances we have missed or the opportunities for joy that have passed us by, as we have waited or sat in a worried huddle. We can, however, decide to look at life and at ourselves, differently.

There is never a time when we are not changing: with every thought, belief and feeling, we are programming our futures. If you, like me, want to find a way past the maze of negative feelings and beliefs with which we punish ourselves, then I hope this short book offers you consolation, support and ideas for your next steps.

HOW ARE YOU?

Ours is a neighbourhood of reserved, polite souls. But take the time to pause while out walking and most folks enjoy a chat. Our first question, "How are you?" is routinely answered, "Fine, thanks" or "not *too* bad," which can mean anything from "I'm feeling really fantastic!" to the less obvious, "Why don't you leave me alone?" We are rarely explicit about how we feel and if, in answer to my polite enquiry, someone was to stop and tell the full truth about their trials and tribulations, I would be taken aback. So we stick with a stoic if rather superficial politeness.

One cold, wet, wintry evening, I was seated in a comfortable room with a group of eight friends. We were huddled up for warmth and the atmosphere was a bit ragged, but convivial. I was looking around, gazing into the depths of a real coal fire, which our host had gone to some trouble to set and light before our arrival. The room was elegant and warm. I was appreciating the comfort of the firm-but-soft chair which enveloped me. However, it seemed that four of my friends had coughs or were recovering from the 'flu. Three others confessed to being in various depths of depression; another said he was endeavouring to put boundaries around his work and do more fun things with his time.

For once I was truly happy. I adore the sight of a beautiful fire and I had weathered tiredness and my short temper to get to a regular gathering which I enjoyed and found deeply rewarding. I felt suddenly at a loss, much like the person in a room who would like to laugh, only to realise that mirth would be in bad taste. Is happiness such a rarity these days or are we perhaps embarrassed to confess it, as if our joy might be considered naïve or unfair? Why do many of us constantly struggle? Do we think this is how to succeed? My puzzlement at such widespread dissatisfaction is what, in part, gave birth to this text and coincidentally to my career as an author. In the midst of a gloomy consensus I yearned to leap up and say, "But surely, you can still recognise the miracle of being alive? Surely you have not all forgotten that happiness is real?"

When I started writing seriously, I had been unhappy for over thirty years and was just beginning my walk towards a more enlightened optimism. It was a challenge I laid down for myself, to flesh out the bones of my cheerfulness with something more substantial which could nourish and help me to grow further into the light. In the weeks, months and years since that spark of hope rose up in my heart and determined to find an outlet, I have continued to reflect on and refine my understandings.

I hope to explore some perspectives which reveal that no matter how tired or sad we are, how overwhelmed or perplexed, there are ways to feel happier. The God(s), the Goddess, Her Upstairs, Jehovah, the Deity, our Sub- or Super-Conscious, the Power in our lives will, naturally, allow struggle. However, before you surrender yourself and all your personal ambitions to a life of hardship, let me reassure you, life does not have to be joyless, loveless and heavy.

This text is for one person at a time: you. It speaks to you *on your own terms*. Here, you do not have to please anyone else, explain why or offer up excuses for what you believe. If it works for you but your friends think you are crazy, how much does that matter? Since we are all different, a wide variety of approaches works well, illuminating truths from different angles.

I hope you discover countless ideas to play with, each as light as a breath of air, as tantalizing as a single shaft of sunlight breaking through heavy clouds on a cold, gloomy day. Any happy thought which touches us can linger a while, illuminating whole new possibilities. Each discovery, unfolding itself, seems to fit with other understandings so easily, that I suspect we are all engaged in assembling pieces of a grand jigsaw which grows daily, expanding in a seamless, logical whole, sweeping through all the everyday assumptions we carry around.

Lessons that I continue to find most helpful naturally reflect those parts of my character and life which provoke on-going challenges. Since we each have different strengths to discover and our own ways of becoming alight to truth, please browse, ponder and cherry-pick the best of what follows. Elements of repetition are not intentional, but confirm my suspicion that each idea is linked, finally, to a central truth: whatever we undertake with joy and sincerity leads us happily into fulfilment and peace.

You may ask: surely, it cannot be so obvious? Actually, one of life's greatest truths is that the things that are good for us, being those things which make us truly happy, *are* simple: there is no hidden agenda, yet we often refuse to believe that *any* straightforward joy is our birth-right. We also expend a great deal of time and energy blindly erecting fences and stumbling blocks to our happiness.

My experiences suggest that changes for the better are more likely to stick around when we build them up slowly, with careful adjustments which we can take on board at our own pace and gently blend with our own style. Rushing into things in the first flush of enthusiasm, I tend to commit too much energy, become overtired and then retreat in a sorry mess, filled with regrets. Though it is not in my nature to wait, reluctantly I have to accept the value of perseverance and success in small steps, the kind of progress that inches forward as I return patiently to repeated positive messages, despite intervening setbacks that seem to want to pull me off course. I am forced to concede that in reshaping my life a sledgehammer approach is often needlessly destructive and painful.

For a gentle change, we can take a tiny seed of an idea, allow it to grow and adapt to suit our particular preferences, then watch it blossom with time, strengthening and becoming as much a part of our lives any of the unhelpful ideas we may have grown up with. Practice and familiarity undoubtedly makes changes easier, but *any small beginning is good enough*.

In setting out the chapters that follow, I attempt to impose boundaries and order, always deceptive, where the natural way is for fluidity, movement and change. The ideas I reflect on naturally blend together, and out in the real world, each scarcely exists separate from the rest. Whether an idea works for you often depends on where you are standing and your direction of travel. But the underlying messages are the same.

Nowhere is there intended to be any sense of

strain, hard work or earnest endeavour. This is not reading to be taken at breakneck speed.

DO YOU LIKE YOUR LIFE?

One view of Life, our greatest gift, is that it is "solitary, poor, nasty, brutish and short" (1). I might also be forgiven for thinking that most adults, whispering in tones quietly conspiratorial, agree that Life is hard therefore must be lived realistically and in a spirit of "quiet desperation" most of the time (2). This dark version of the way we see things is even awarded royal respect. Notice how we shield our children carefully from the realities of life – because we think that they hurt – gradually awakening them to life's "truths" as they get older. Let the little ones enjoy their childhood while they can, we say, because life sure is hell when you are grown up.

Growing older does appear to be widely viewed as a prescription for the ritual introduction of disappointments. Hearing encouraging words such as, "No", "Stop it" or "You can't, because…" as we grow older, it is little wonder that many of us feel grey around the gills and chronically depressed. On the other hand, as children accumulate years, they seem to feel increasingly pressured to be "terribly grown up", while, in deference to their clear skin and youthful looks, we who are older hide the signs of passing time with a plethora of personal grooming products and cosmetic procedures, so terrified are we that old age means decrepitude, loneliness and isolation. For too many of us, this becomes a reality which the cult of youth reinforces.

These are not very *helpful* views of life, are they? Why should growing older not be understood as a gentle process of unfolding, during which we discover the true meaning of peace, serenity and acceptance? I have never been happier than I am today, mainly because I now see ageing as an opportunity to bring perseverance, optimism and faith to the forefront of my life and allow them to work wonders every day.

Many people I meet assume that I am unfortunate. They ask me, with concern in every gesture, "So what happened to you, then?" and if I am not very careful I could get drawn back into a world of regretful introspection and be defined once again by my strange limping and my tendency to fall over. But I refuse to go back down that path, because returning to the painful assumptions of yesteryear makes me feel small, helpless, a victim of fate with no escape. These are horrible and dark beliefs to live with. Apart from any other consideration, whenever I forget and, from force of habit, revert to looking at life through the scratched lenses called "hardship", I get dog tired. Deep in my heart, I know that tiredness is what I feel when I am moving the wrong way and in the wrong direction.

To be in any degree content, I find that I must stifle any belief which assumes that *of course* life consists of a series of bitter trials and disappointments through which I must stumble as if through a desert, gasping. Sometimes, I have to admit, a scan around my local gym does make me wonder: the room is regularly filled to overflowing with a sweating, seemingly desperate clientele, who appear to be in considerable pain. In the midst of our affluence, we seem to nourish an inbuilt desire for suffering, as if without our daily dose of pain we feel only half alive.

It *is* true that without suffering we cannot know how it feels *not* to suffer. Unless we visit despair we may never discover what bliss feels like. We all look back on hard times which have helped us to appreciate our successes and be thankful for the progress we have made. "Good" and "bad" times are most helpful when we appreciate them as two halves which make our lives a whole experience.

If you consider that your life is vile because your partner of twenty years went off with your best friend or you have just lost your job, I sincerely hope you do not consider me hurtful if I maintain that, despite its ups and downs, the gift of life is precious. If you hail from the school of hard knocks and incline to the view that life is naturally painful and we are all fools who think otherwise, perhaps I can throw some more light your way. If your life is hard, who is it hurting?

My husband has gone out this winter evening, leaving me alone. It is Friday, yet he has to drive my daughter halfway across the country to take her to a kiddies' party. He may fit in an hour of work at his office, before collecting Seline and her friend for the return journey.

Meanwhile, on the home front, I am ill with a stomach complaint and hungry after two days of nausea and rather reluctant fasting. Neither the central heating nor my internet connection is working. Rather than offering to cook something tempting and delicious, rather than phoning a plumber or the computer engineer and hoping to arrange a home visit, Eddie has left me alone in a chilly flat with an empty fridge: Friday night offers slim pickings. Even my television is only showing two decent channels. Excuse me, while I have a tantrum. I'll be right back.

Some of what follows may have you stomping across the room in a fury, wanting to ring me up and say, "Look, you moron!" Yeah, I know. I am sorry if it all sounds trite and simplistic. Kids, work and mortgages are all serious business and if, in the midst of changing nappies, making a meal to suit several tastes and answering a knock at the front door, someone were to waft past me in a caftan murmuring, "Hang loose, take it easy…" I would find it hard to stay calm too. But being upset makes me unwell; and I hate to get my energy from the adrenalin rush of anger. Anger keeps us going but is best used short-term, not as a habitual response to life's injustices.

Physically exhausted and mentally challenged, in the early years of child-rearing I developed many coping strategies. One of these was to agree, well, if I can't face the prospect of a whole day of this, I can cope for a couple of hours. If that is too much, I could at least manage half an hour; and if that is too long, how about the next ten minutes? If that is still daunting, the next ten seconds should be just about manageable. It worked. Heavy feelings lifted off my shoulders and I immediately felt much lighter and freer.

This book asks, "How do you feel?" and helps you to find ways to honour your feelings and use their energy productively. We cannot feel happy while the whole gamut of our emotions lies overlooked and forgotten. As part of a process of starting again – and again and again – take any idea that appeals to you and use it as you wish, in *any positive* variation that helps you *feel better*. If you feel as if you have never been very happy or you think a cheerful life is just not for you, then you might try experimenting with being happy for five minutes. If that is too long, set your target for two minutes, two seconds or any small space that brings relief. After the first time, it becomes easier to say, "Well, another five minutes of this might be nice…"

Quite by accident, I have discovered that vocalization (call it singing if you like) helps me to access feelings that may be buried deep. So if you are not sure how you feel; if something is annoying you but you don't know what; or if you are fed up or feeling "blah", try giving voice to *something*. Singing can help you be clearer about your mood and unearth what may be bugging you or even help clarify what you would like to do next. With the aim of feeling better, voice whatever sound comes to you, happy or sad and whether or not you like singing. Singing also helps to bypass our mental reluctance, making it easier for us not only to locate sources of unease intuitively, but also to overcome these more easily without attracting hostile reactions. Any songful noise works. Try it!

If we have spent a lifetime blocking out our feelings, it can be a challenge to unearth them and begin listening to them again. Feelings often lie buried deep, lost to us beneath years of "coping" and "managing". We smother emotions exactly as if we are ashamed of them and indeed, if we have denied anger and frustration for decades, it is quite likely that we would fear unleashing a deluge of destruction if we ever began being honest. Yet, refusing to acknowledge our feelings only gives them more power and momentum. When feelings are allowed space to express themselves freely, with practice and patience, they become our allies and can form a strong and reliable compass which helps to guide our steps.

EMOTIONAL HONESTY

We all have occasions when our normally placid exterior cracks and instead of being peaceful, calm and accommodating of everything from "courtesy" telephone callers to our children's incessant demands while we are trying to eat a meal, we hiss and spit like a volcanic inferno. When we are feeling less than saintly, emotional honesty helps greatly to lessen the knock-on effects of negative feelings such as anger, sadness and frustration. So, do we rant and rave or do we shove all that bad feeling down into our stomachs and just pretend we are fine, thank you? Personally, I'm with the "howl and get it over with" school of thought.

When our children pester us to play with them do we say, "Later dear, not just now"? Unhappy with our answer, they raise the volume, repeat their questions and dance around us more wildly, until we set down what we are doing and finally look them in the eye. "All right, what do you want? Would you like us to play?" When we give children our wholehearted attention for as long as they wish, they soon go off happily by themselves, secure in the knowledge that we have listened to them.

Our feelings are like our children. They never leave us and live loyally within us, often overlooked and forgotten as we rush about getting things done. We think, as we grow older, find a path and follow it, that we can leave our feelings behind, but they stay with us. When we can't find the words to express what we feel, our emotions, which may have remained unexpressed since before we could talk, come to the surface.

Though it is often necessary and expedient to suppress negative feelings in particular situations – we would be out of a job if we told our lousy managers what we really thought of them – constantly denying unhappiness makes it linger and turn up the volume until we give it some proper attention. We put off dealing with negativity or lousy office politics for hours, days, weeks, months and years. Eventually, all that emotion comes home and demands a hearing.

A storm of pent-up frustration we unleash may be spectacular, but once we become reacquainted with our honest feelings, we probably notice that other people are relieved we have stopped pretending *everything is fine, thank you!* when it obviously isn't. A storm of protest in answer to our honestly expressed feelings is unlikely. Believe it or not, emotional honesty is usually met with silence or approval. Accepting how we feel makes us less ashamed, so given time, the negative fallout of our anger or frustration is usually short-lived. When I accept my sadness, frustration or anger and allow myself to feel them deeply, they are more likely to feel very intense for a while, then go *cleanly* away, leaving me in peace. After a storm, the air clears and smells sweet again. Conversely, fully allowing myself to feel and express positive emotions fills me with delightful, healthy energy that grows as it is shared and benefits everyone.

Just as being honest about our feelings is beneficial, expressing our choices clearly is very empowering; and I speak as one who knows. As a self-confessed doormat, I sat around being nice and obliging, never saying "no" for fear of upsetting everyone, although in giving away most of my time and energy, I became very unhappy and resentful. I did not often make positive choices either, because I believed that my choices were rather pointless. Sitting around aimlessly, my time was taken up helping to sort out other people's problems – though I'm not sure I was a great deal of help. Failing to spend my time – my life! – doing what I chose, other people's concerns filled in huge amounts of my space, which became very frustrating for them and for me. I'm not blaming them, incidentally. This is just how Life works and even then, I knew that others didn't like my passivity any more than I did. They got fed up choosing for me, making up my mind for me and being expected to hold me up while I dithered.

How might my life have worked out better, if I had had the courage to express my feelings and choices clearly? Instead of living a half-life overshadowed by crummy compromises, lack of resources and strife, I might have had fun. Yet it took me many years to finally pluck up the courage to express myself clearly, even about something as simple as whether I enjoyed watching football.

Respecting our choices while being friendly and open towards the needs and expectations of others, we may feel we are setting ourselves up for a whole lot of conflict. But in fact, our friends love us more when we do what we prefer, without always relying on them, and our lives fall more easily into line. Who wants to be leaned on all the time?

Doreen Virtue writes, "A good rule of thumb for how to spend your time is to never do anything you don't want to do" (3). Once we are comfortable with agreeing, "Yes, I would like that very much," or "Actually, I can't manage on Tuesday, I have a prior appointment..." we can go a step beyond reserving some personal "quality time" and begin reclaiming *all* the time in our lives for ourselves, which, is what

I think Doreen Virtue means. It is neither selfish nor unkind to reframe life in this way. If we first accept that we reclaim all our time and *then* choose to be giving, kind or patient, our time remains fundamentally our own, though most of us naturally go on to do many things for and with others. Since we start out seeing ourselves as master of our choices, resentment, tiredness, "white lies" and impatience gradually fade away.

If you know you fight after a drink, stop drinking. If you can't stand your neighbour, stop speaking to him unless he is more considerate. If you hate "family Sundays" because you do all the cooking and row afterwards, go to your favourite restaurant for lunch instead. If you hate Christmas, ignore it. If you are sick and tired of it all, change your routine. If you don't like doing a thing you can possibly escape, don't do it.

GET OUT OF YOUR GROOVE

In her book "Excuse Me, Your Life is Waiting" (4) Lynn Grabhorn highlighted the value of cutting away from our bad habits and feelings as soon as possible after something upsets us. Unless we master the "quick stop" we may find that our whole day is spoiled by one small thing going wrong, which is particularly true for me first thing in the morning.

When small bad habits or irritations threaten to unhinge a peaceful day, we stop them in their tracks by changing the subject immediately, before the internal arguments escalate. Honesty helps us to admit that we may have set off doing something we would like to stop: "Yeah, I really am tired, actually. I think I'll go back to bed after all…" We can retrace our steps, leave the room, go out for a walk or take a shower.

Jumping from your groove is not about pretending that everything is wonderful when it obviously isn't. It is about quickly noticing the immediate effect that old, grinding habits have and refusing to get sidetracked or sucked down by them into the usual round of complaints and irritation. Refusing to get pulled down into unhelpful situations is a significant part of how we choose to express our autonomy and often overlooked. Our tendency to get pulled down by the repetitive voices of duty and necessity is often reinforced by the many rational, sensible explanations we school ourselves with, ("people are expecting me to do this", "my family are depending on me", "we always go shopping at this time") which often make a virtue of ignoring our feelings, just when it would be most helpful to acknowledge them. Being authentic about how we feel allows us to step away from our usual patterns and turn down the volume on those that no longer serve us.

Do we grumble every morning? Are Saturdays punctuated by complaints? Does Dad get a bucket-load of unhappiness when he comes home at the end of the day? Are repeating patterns of fear and unhappiness spoiling my opportunities? Do I want to let go of a bad habit that has upset me every morning for the last twenty years? Yes! My heart is willing, but habits are strong...

A groove can be rather difficult to jump out of. A groove isn't a groove unless it is a physical dip, which can be deep if we have been going around in it for a while, each circuit digging us down a little further. Grooves also happen in the brain, where they have their uses, allowing us to do routine tasks without a lot of thought and freeing up our minds to think about other, more interesting matters. But faced with unchanging routines, it can take a jump or a shove to shift our thoughts and behaviour out to somewhere else.

If this sounds like you, make a positive choice: if you honestly feel like resting, go back to bed and relax for a while. Decide to start again. If housework is depressing, go outside, run to the park in the rain, go and visit friends, put on some music, have a party, dance on the kitchen table or paint a picture. Throw out the dead house plants that you feel guilty about every time you walk past them – which has been for some years now… Do you get the idea?

LIFE IS A MIRROR

I am constantly reminded that my every thought, every word I utter and all the things I do, quickly bounce right back to me: if I happen to smirk rather unkindly at someone and stride past them with my nose in the air, I trip and find myself flat on my face while they walk on by.

I never used to understand what was going on. These days I am more willing to see this as an example of "instant Karma" because I rather playfully believe that Her Upstairs is keeping my account neatly balanced and up-to-date. I am grateful. I am lucky. I have someone keeping an eye out for me; and their constant nudges remind me to stay centred in kindness and love.

I often forget that what someone does for or to me is a reflection of what I am doing for or to them. Each day I rediscover that the adage, "Do unto others what you would like them to do to you," is not flippant moralizing, but a reminder that If I am hoping for a peaceful, fruitful or meaningful life, I can be the one who sets the ball rolling. For example, whenever we are motivated by love, our actions are automatically blessed and will bring benefits to all, regardless of whether we can see any immediate purpose in what we are doing.

It seems that, without much giving the matter a great deal of thought, the largest majority of us hold beliefs and thoughts which emphasize our helplessness. Cornered by necessity, hardship and financial stringency, we often perceive the forces that shape our world as being immensely more inevitable and powerful than we are…Many of us grow into a mindset which accepts without question that "what happens to us" is simply the way the World works, much more real and convincing than anything we do for ourselves to influence any outcomes. Our behaviour then tends to strengthen our belief that we are forced to react to what is happening to us, a cycle which can repeat endlessly while we clutch at straws and ask, "Why?"

Seen from this perspective, life often feels less than powerful, less than free and less than happy. Many of us appear to live reactively, which may be one reason why we often find ourselves searching continuously, if not obsessively, for answers to questions such as, "What is life for?", "Why is life so hard?" or "What on Earth am I doing here?" The world of reactive living is not very fruitful: as we do not see ourselves actively shaping our destiny, we often react defensively or fearfully. When we base our choices on whatever life throws our way or what others "do to us", we see only half of the picture.

I used to wake up each day and, because the weather is often grey, windy and wet around here, I would mutter darkly, "Drat! Another miserable day. What a shame to get out of bed. I am *fed up* with this crummy life…" Somehow, after a bad start I noticed that my day didn't pick up from there. I found one-hundred-and-one things going wrong and most of what I did felt incredibly tiring. Or before I've even woken up properly, I'm automatically thinking about what my daughter needs, what my husband is doing. To take another example, I might become accustomed to the pattern of thought that says, "I'm depressed because of this, that or the next piece of stuff – garbage, crap, difficult shit – going on in my life right now."

But wait a moment. Why did it take me so long to realise that I can think and act differently? No matter what jobs I have on my list for today, I can choose how I feel while I am doing these. No matter how awful things are or what has happened to me – and I've had some months and years that have felt like a march over rough desert in bare feet – I can still choose to be happy anyway and experience the whole of my life differently. If something does not work out the way I expect it to, or if something upsetting comes along, sure, I can get upset for a while. But eventually, I have to choose, and the best way to make the most of my time here is finally to accept the outcome, learn from it and move on.

What I choose to believe – am I powerful or weak, am I upset or amused? – is as much part of me as the clothes I wear each day. Though there will inevitably be times when we feel sad or discouraged, a clear decision to follow through with what we prefer is immensely rewarding. As we decide for ourselves, it becomes increasingly evident we can exercise endless beneficial choices that nurture us and deepen our sense of self-worth.

So let us see what happens when I run that first scenario again. This time I decide to wake gently; and I willingly select "happiness" from the choices on offer. After all, I am in my warm, comfortable bed. Deliberately stretching a smile across my face (because a smile feels better than a flat grimace) I soon feel warm contentment, instead of the edgy dissatisfaction of being half-dead awake. I decide to snuggle down under the quilt for another ten minutes of blissful peace. Then I hear footsteps and see the head of my daughter pop round the end of the bed. She is pretty, with untidy hair bouncing in unruly curls around her face. I cannot help smiling at her morning joy: energy fizzes all around her. She opens the bedroom curtains and beyond them I see a grey, wet and cold day, which looks much the same as yesterday and the day before.

I could complain, I could do that so easily. But no! I am in charge around here, therefore I notice shards of light breaking bravely through dark clouds, waking me up gently…It is a good day, after all. Where would we be without rain?

This morning I allow myself to feel good about dozing a while longer. I call it freedom, rather than laziness, knowing that when I wake up more gently, my good mood tends to stay around all day. Waiting twenty minutes, I use my time to look forward to a great morning, enjoying the freedom to paint any picture I desire and do anything I like. I feel real gratitude.

None of these mental exercises is hard, but they do take a certain mindful discipline and focus, especially after a lifetime of complaining. How refreshing happy thoughts are any time of day. I sing in the shower and my daughter joins in, which makes me laugh. I decide that yes, indeed, today is a great day, the best day of my life. It is the only day I have to play with. Having anchored my intention to feel good, the "up" feeling just stays around.

Abruptly I remember, with a lurch in my stomach, that my neighbour walked past me yesterday without saying hello. I feel sure she is avoiding me, because she heard me losing it big time on Wednesday and she hasn't forgotten the sounds of my raging curses and weeping. I pause to reflect that maybe I really am a bad tempered so-and-so and deserve to be thoroughly embarrassed. As soon as that thought enters my head, things go wrong. Small upsets, the same size as my doubts, crop up like pins, drawn to me by my fretfulness: I get an ache in my chest. I drop a box of work papers and bump my head on an open drawer while I am bending to retrieve them from the kitchen floor; I suddenly feel tired and think I may be getting a headache. I trip over the vacuum flex which gets tangled around my ankles.

Then, as if stepping out of myself, I realise what is happening and before the negativity escalates, I gently stop and say, "Well, who cares? I forgave myself a while ago. I was really yelling at me and that certainly didn't help, so let's just forget it, shall we? The sooner I let go of that memory, the better. My downstairs neighbour is perfectly civil to me – I am okay!" With a deliberate intention to feel better and move forward, I pick up my mood, get dressed in warm clothes to suit the weather, eat a good breakfast and chat with my daughter as we decide what we would like to do today. Before we go out I easily manage a whole week's worth of housework in just over an hour. I feel great and the rest of the day is happy and productive.

I used to worry if I hadn't been shopping for a week or ten days. I was sure we would go hungry and the fridge always seemed to be empty. I recall forlornly contemplating half-finished jars of mayonnaise and old jugs of milk. Now, because it makes me feel better, I have started saying, "There is lots of food in my kitchen. The fridge and the cupboards are full. Meals are easy to find and fun to prepare." I expect to have enough. These days, on the few evenings I cannot think what to cook, I reassure myself that "abundance is everywhere," and I almost always find a meal. I often ask for help with what to prepare, and answers pop into my head. As I invite solutions, they come to me.

Personally, I have come by slow degrees to accept that life works better when I do not struggle, push and shove through life, as if I were hacking at a thicket of thorns with a puny knife. The more I push and shove, the more resistance I place in the way of solutions reaching me. I find that worrying, and trying to think myself out of trouble, rarely succeeds. Hard, cold, rains will come, but instead of muttering curses and frowning I can choose to bless the rain, seeing it as another opportunity to do something different and experiment with different choices. If the way forward is unclear, I can stay centred in peace, until a solution becomes clear. When I relax, I find that good flows towards me, unimpeded by labouring doubts.

When I was in office employment, I tolerated the work but the politics fitted me like a badly-tailored dress. I dreaded every day and felt a grudge – or maybe it was a heavy despair – the size of my desk. Now I realise that I was unable to bring sufficient creativity to my work and the pressures of the job got me down. I had endurance, and spent many hours reading files and drafting papers, but I thought the system was defective and had decided it was dreadful, so of course it didn't work for me. That's hardly surprising: I never asked or expected it to.

What may read as a belated apology is really the acknowledgement that I wasn't doing myself or my colleagues any favours. I was full of frustration, doubt and fear. But instead of admitting how I felt and allowing myself to go away and have a bit of fun, I was challenging; and challenges came back at me by the bucket-load.

If your life is unrewarding, a hassle, depressing or if you just seem to mess up continually, now is the time to change your mind: choose what you would like to do or feel now. Whether you are aware of it or not, simply by existing, your body exudes a power, rather like a radio that is permanently switched on. You cannot turn the power off, though you can drown out the signal with worry and frantic activity. Why not use all that lovely energy for your own benefit, by deliberately selecting thoughts, beliefs, words and activities that feel good?

Behaviours to avoid if you don't want to get needlessly hurt include gossiping, continual criticism, sarcasm, complaining, making unfair comparisons, being late or discourteous, holding grudges, being continually angry, cross, judgmental, stubborn or not listening. Such behaviours forge heavy rods over our backs, making our precious time needlessly difficult. When we use our power in the wrong way, it usually comes back to hurt us. Choose any image you like to remind you that what you throw out comes back, either to haunt or comfort you.

Imagine you know a man at work who is fairly new to his job. Let's call him Joe. One morning, while making light conversation, you say something like, "Lovely socks, Joe, would I suit them too, d'you think?" the kind of joke or informal comment that other colleagues might not even notice. Your new workmate, however, reacts as if he has been bitten by a cobra and from the look on his face it is obvious that he feels deeply aggrieved. Joe responds with a volley of words, a real attack on you. Is he being overly sensitive? Maybe he is very fond of his bright pink Scooby Doo socks which were a present from his lover, in which case you would hopefully apologise and move on.

Perhaps Joe is very aware of what you said, but took up your words in a way that you did not intend, as personal criticism. If he reacts forcefully all the time, his life at work eventually becomes unbearable because he perceives all statements in a critical light, as attack. He sees the world as a hostile place, therefore it is. I speak about this scenario with some authority, because for more years than I care to remember, I was like Joe. I never saw the joke, because it felt as though the joke was on me.

In this example it is a fair guess that Joe attacks you because he thinks you are being hostile, even though you were extending the hand of friendship. Next time, presumably, you will be more wary. Poor Joe is living *as* if the world is hostile and suffering. Eventually, the world *does* become hostile to him, because he is morbidly sensitive to criticism and people just get fed up. Either way, in his reality the world is a hard place.

These are small examples and we may not think that what we do makes much difference; but the best place to notice the impact of our every choice is here and now, with our own minutes and days. Each loving thought, each thoughtful action, makes a difference.

CELL MEMORY

One Wednesday afternoon I was working in the kitchen. I was cooking supper, while at the kitchen table my daughter was happily playing with a paper theatre that stood propped up. Figures of cut-out mice lay scattered among paper and crayons.

Suddenly I felt myself growing tense and cross. Out of the blue, I felt stressed and unhappy. Thankfully, I caught my mood in time and was able to examine it. Instead of getting louder and taking it out on my girl, I asked, "Were on Earth has this come from? I know this doesn't happen on a Monday, Tuesday, Thursday, Friday or at the weekend... What's happening? Help!"

The answer came to me as clear as a bell: "*The memory is in your cells*".

Well now! What on earth does that mean?

Well...Wednesday *used to be* a difficult day for me. Everything happens on a Wednesday, which is fatal for my perfectionist tendencies. In the midst of Everything, a fishmonger comes to my door in the late afternoon. If I am not at home, he leaves a couple of haddock fillets on the doorstep, which is very thoughtful of him. I look forward to seeing him. These days it is a pleasure, though it *used to be* a bit of a chore.

Because I was unable to carry her, I had to leave my baby daughter on her own in our first-floor flat while I scampered as fast as I could down the stairs and back without seeming to be rude in my haste. By four o'clock when I was faced with the task of preparing supper, I was so tired and strung out that I would burn the fish, spoil the food and ruin the pot. After all that effort, there would be nothing for us to eat, a ruined pan *and* a bad smell that would linger for days afterwards, reminding me of my failure. Twice I had to purchase new kitchenware. I was not a pretty sight by six o'clock on a Wednesday evening.

Although such events as these last took place over four years ago and I had totally forgotten them, it was scenes of chaos and upset like these that my body was recalling on that otherwise tranquil and trouble-free afternoon. The theory of cell memory suggests that every cell in our body remembers what happens and stores the memories of our reactions to any situation.

While to my logical mind it sounds completely mad, this theory would indeed explain why I was getting stressed about nothing. Even though I was no longer consciously aware of it, my body was reacting to Wednesday afternoons as difficult: I was reacting to stress that was no longer there.

When I realised this might explain how I was feeling, I leapt in the air and danced! Even if it is only a crazy idea, "cell memory" could help to explain a lot about the difficulties we face when we decide to change our lives. We may be thinking better thoughts and taking all the right steps in a new direction but, at a subconscious level, we are lumbered with old reactions and feelings based on memories long forgotten. The mind reacts using the information it already has, even if that information is well out of date. What happened to me suggests that cell memory is very strong.

Straightaway I decided, "Okay, then, let's make NEW cell memories – Wednesdays are great fun! I don't need to make fish pie on Wednesdays ever again. Actually, I hate fish pie! Thank God I can cook something different." Knowing that there was something I could do to help myself, I heaved a sigh of relief and made a point of "changing the record". Hopefully, with time, my body's memories of Wednesday afternoon are becoming re-educated into something more cheerful.

Cell memory might also explain why we sometimes react strongly when we feel that someone is "pressing our buttons". We wonder what could trigger sudden explosive rage or profound unhappiness. Perhaps the mind is recalling a similar set of events and trotting out an old response. There is no guarantee that our oldest response is the best one.

In that case we can reassure ourselves and repeat to ourselves often, that now is NEW. Now is fresh and different. Now is better. Now is how I want it to be and I can change my attitude to what is happening now. Even if none of these statements is true, I feel better when I repeat them. That alone is sometimes enough.

Perhaps I am a stressed single mother with two children, scraping a living on benefits and with no hope of getting the wonderful job of my dreams. If I say, "I have a wonderful job which pays me great money and I work for people whom I love and respect," instantly I feel better. I sit up straighter and smile because, said with an ounce of feeling, these words fill my heart with renewed hope and happiness. For a moment I feel strong. If I keep reminding myself of this, I am immediately on the lookout to discover all the ways in which this truth is reality in my life: I recognise that the work I do with and for my children is the best and the most important job in the world. I enjoy the dream that one day, I may discover new ways to turn my hopes into reality.

Isn't this kind of self-belief better than having a good old moan? If I wish to believe that I never amount to anything and no-one appreciates how hard I work, if I repeat these words with emotion, there are no prizes for guessing how I feel at the end of the day. Give yourself a break and give your mind, your body and all your cells a health workout with some crazily positive re-invention – anything will do.

AFFIRMING WHAT WE CHOOSE

One way to reconfigure our views on life is to use positive statements – which some of us call "affirmations" – as often as possible, until they become a beneficial habit, part of a new, helpful routine. You may have heard the word "mantras" but most of us are not eastern yogis and there is no reason to make something fancy out of a mere re-arrangement in our perspective: an affirmation is an *acknowledgement of a positive, helpful truth as part of our (new) reality.*

For best results, affirmations are most effective when spoken in the present tense. They are best taken as an opportunity to lightly notice, perhaps for the first time, that what we are stating is tantalizingly true. If spoken as a future hope or expectation, affirmations are unlikely to help. For example, there is no point in saying, "I am going to be happy, when…" Similarly, saying, "I am not scared" is unhelpful since that phrase brings to mind a fear we are trying to distance ourselves from. Experiment with, "I am confident and happy", "Everything that happens in my life is a blessing for me" or, "I accept prosperity into my life and welcome blessings with open arms."

It is fun experimenting with various words and phrases until we find something we enjoy the sound of. Consider any prospect that feels good, punch in some feeling and then repeat it until you recognise it is true.

How do you react to the following statements?

~ Life is abundant and I am part of life.

~ Therefore I happily receive abundant love and joyous friendship, rewarding work, bundles of fun, pleasure, laughter, excitement, plenty of money, the whole delicious experience of having everything I desire.

~ I welcome gifts into my life.

~ I see abundance everywhere and it is for me.

~ There is plenty for everyone.

~ Success comes easily to me.

~ My life is wonderful.

~ I am beautiful.

~ I love myself now, today and always, no matter what I do.

~ I welcome love and joy into my life.

- I deserve to be happy.
- I am powerful.
- My every thought creates my future.
- I am alive, therefore I am lovable.
- Whatever I am doing, the Universe always supports me.
- The Universe always works to procure the best outcome for me.

Positive affirmations spoken perhaps for the first time may sound very unusual, almost like a foreign language. They often produce an emotional reaction after the first few times spoken aloud. With the intention of changing the way we see things, when we speak a new, positive affirmation which turns our usual understanding of the world upside down, first we may giggle, thinking this is just a silly game. If we push past our disbelief and embarrassment and repeat our chosen words with feeling and conviction, we may find ourselves reacting with considerable negative emotion: mounting incredulity, annoyance, sadness, frustration or anger. I used to catch myself muttering, "This is all such nonsense, how ridiculous!" and there are times when small, simple, innocent affirmations like "I love and cherish myself" or "I deserve beautiful clothes" make me weep.

If I declare, "My body is beautiful", I am going against forty years of unhelpful messages to myself about how ugly I am, how ungainly, how awful and so on... Though these distortions in my self-image lie hidden, they are deeply ingrained. For example, in many social situations, I hide my hands, folding my fingers out of the way, which might be because I have been so ashamed of biting my nails. Even though this problem is finally receding, it takes patience, acceptance and often lots of time, to undo unhelpful messages from the past.

Extra help is at hand: singing affirmations is doubly powerful. Not only do we remember what we sing far more clearly and for far longer than what we talk about – children love to learn through singing rhymes – but singing is effective to bypass mental hostility and self-doubt. For some reason, the human experience is much gentler when it is sung through, so if you encounter difficulty with any of this, try finding phrases to sing or chant with instead.

Gradually, our positive beliefs about ourselves feel ever truer, and as we feel them true we don't need to say them as much as believe them and sing them powerfully. Our beliefs and the changing inner landscape of self-empowerment can nurture us in sound or in dignified silence whatever we are doing.

Every single positive message, feeling or belief is valuable to help overcome negativity. As I love myself more, I am less ashamed of my bitten hands and learn to accept them as they are. Because I am less ashamed of my weaknesses, I bite my nails less often, so there is less to be ashamed of. Thus I see improvements and am encouraged to continue with them.

If a statement of hope such as, "I welcome lots of joy and laughter into my life" brings up feelings of anger, you may wish to explore why that might be. After all, love and laughter are everyone's birth-right. *Observe* negative emotions as they arise, rather than buying into them. Louise Hay (5) reminds us repeatedly that negative reactions are very helpful, since they reveal our weaknesses, what we are frightened of, and the occasions when persisting with positive changes are most beneficial.

We believe and accept the power of positive affirmations when we recognise – at last – that the process of life, the way it moves us forward and unfolds for us, always works within a perfect scheme to maximise the potential of everything we offer, and that we deserve to share in that perfection, because we are also perfectly made and allowed to live happily as we are. Finally, it percolates through age-old stiffness that all of the above statements are true and we are much better off when we accept them gently.

If happiness still sounds like a tall order – pretend. Even when I have to go out into the world armed with a counterfeit grin, I feel better. When we smile, our minds are fooled into thinking something wonderful is going on and we feel happier. Many people swear by the healing effects of laughter, even to the extent of curing illnesses such as depression, anxiety and cancer. Conversely, how many ailments are caused by lingering and hidden unhappiness?

MEDITATION AND VISUALIZATION

I am still recovering from a life-long belief that "sitting doing nothing" is a waste of time. These days I love the freedom of doing nothing and in the process I have discovered visualization and meditation techniques. With a bit of open-ness and practice, meditation and visualization, which include daydreaming, waking dreams and night dreams, have become welcome, faithful friends, very helpful in guiding and informing my choices.

Like dreams, these processes are intensely personal and what we gain from them depends very much on our individual tastes and characters. For me, meditation is about calming and eventually excluding the noisy thoughts and preoccupations that constantly flit through my head. I am not always able to access the silence but when I do, simple peace can go very deep; and when I trust it, the resulting calm is immensely helpful, not solely to recharge my batteries, but also for letting in new awareness which would otherwise struggle to be noticed.

There are countless ways to meditate. Experiment with meditative sitting, walking, standing, singing or chanting, visualization, guided visualization, writing, creative arts, even compiling jigsaws: anything that allows you to set aside your noisy mind and centre down.

Give yourself permission to experiment. Find a quiet place where you love *to be*. If this is all new to you, I suggest starting with a few minutes, so that anticipation and enthusiasm keep you company all the way. You may feel that a few moments are enough, until you get used to the feeling of silence. Gradually increase the length of time you choose to spend in quietness. With practice, the only equipment you need is a decision to begin and willingness to be still.

When I started listening in the early days, one time I was all set up in a quiet room, a space bathed by the early morning sun and with the telephone unplugged. I had a long free morning and in my enthusiasm had made a start immediately after a very quick breakfast. Suddenly I felt very hungry and I knew I was being told that I should go and have a beautiful and plentiful meal, because that would honour the process. Hints such as these are solely for our benefit and we are greatly rewarded when we listen and follow them. So I went through to the kitchen and fetched down a beautiful blue plate, placing on it lots of small portions of different, colourful, delicious food. Making a small ceremony of it, I said thank you and ate with relish. I returned to the living-room and had one of my best meditation sessions ever.

I try to clear away commitments for at least an hour. It also helps if I set aside a certain time each day for my contemplation and pencil that into my calendar so that I respect the space for this activity. Otherwise, I would find one-hundred-and-one other things to do, which is strange, considering how much I enjoy peaceful dreaming. After some trial and error I have decided I still prefer mornings after breakfast, when I am least likely to fall sleep. Choosing a sunny spot, I sit relaxed and, with my eyes closed I concentrate on an image of something or nothing. We can explore any thought, picture or place we wish and see beauty in all the details that the mind's eye conjures: a bank of fragrant blooms in a rose garden, a beautiful angel, a luxurious piece of cloth… any image which makes us feel calm, loved and wrapped in warmth. I look forward to being free: free to dream of what I love best. What a fantastic feeling!

When I wish to get to a level faster, I focus on a point in the middle of my forehead. Please don't feel this "has" to work for you: I discovered it by accident. I aim to get into a place where there is a great pool of light and comfortable peace. David Wells (6) takes a shower before his spiritual work, but I could not – my skin would dry up like a prune. However, I liked the idea and now I include a variety of cleansing images in many of my sessions.

Visualization is also meditation, though, to my way of thinking, it more directly connects with admitting visual beauty. I give myself permission to take a profoundly restful journey, talk to any person I wish and have experiences in my imagination that lead me anywhere: I dwell in the realms of colour and music, the smells and the sounds of the seaside, the primeval forests or the mountaintops.

My usual visualization these days is a swim anywhere I fancy to wash away the concerns of the moment, (the hot springs of Iceland or a tropical paradise, anyone?) followed by a ritual robing which is my acknowledgement that this visualization is special and beautiful. I may take a walk through an archway to a fragrant garden, a field of growing barley, the beach, a glade or a wide circle of trees. Sometimes, Spirit lends a hand, showing me things or taking me to unexpected places, where I learn something new or gain insight into a question that is waiting to be answered. I sometimes find myself in a place I never planned, but which fits my current desires exactly.

I keep a dream diary and have done so for many years. I do not fill it in every day, but it has its place at my bedside; and in it I record dreams, coincidences or images I receive, – the ones that *I know* are important – or which are bringing me messages. Any dream will have an impact on what I do, regardless of whether I can remember it or not. But even so, I love unearthing unexpected meanings and contexts and for that, a dream journal is so valuable. It also becomes easier to notice recurring themes which have special meanings for us. In my personal dictionary, an archway is the top half of a circle, which is a symbol for me of movement, power, change and completion. The archway is shown in different ways: short or tall, a wide arch or a small doorway; it may be composed of different elements, wood, marble, rocks, trees, stones, swept up leaves, shimmering light. It becomes clearer to me that even the type of arch and the details evident in the state of repair of walls or surfaces carry meaning: the smallest details are instructive.

Into the stillness we can ask, "What would you like me to know?" Prefacing our silence with a question helps develop our ability to wait expectantly. What we hear may depend on how well we listen. If we would like help with a specific issue, we may start with an admission that, "I feel sad, today" – or "I feel at a loss about X. I would really like some help with this". *Please do not feel that you have to follow a format.* I return to several themes regularly. I am comfortable basing my visualizations around familiar images, because I have found over the years that they hold particular meanings for me.

Favourite images include:

- ~ Gates and paths, perhaps leading to a field or fields;
- ~ Single trees of all kinds and forests of trees;
- ~ A swim in a pool or at the beach, followed by a walk;
- ~ People we meet when we are walking along or who come with a message for us;
- ~ Motor vehicles and their state of repair;
- ~ Buildings, their position in the landscape, their condition.

Allowing these processes to reveal pictures or impressions, subtle truths are gradually uncovered. By careful degrees, I gain the impression that I am being offered a gift. I begin to trust the process to reveal to me, in the way that will best enable me to understand, the next steps in the journey or the answers to questions that may be plaguing me. I may choose to sit in a pool of white light and silence, waiting for what may come. I may see picture metaphors; at other times I could swear I "hear" a voice speaking. The first time I heard a voice it took me quite by surprise.

Meditation also teaches patience. All things are

revealed in their proper time and in the best way for us to take them on board and make good use of them. This freedom to ask questions and wait peacefully for answers is available to each one of us and when I meditate regularly, I feel as if I am tapping into the wisdom of ages.

I only speak from my own experience which has demonstrated repeatedly that the power of visualization comes from the vividness and richness of the colours and the imagery I am blessed with, combined with the deep emotional impact of what I see and discover. I have had messages in the form of pictures with multiple meanings and puns. The vividness of the colours makes these messages almost impossible to forget.

For example, when I was a teenager I had a dream in the form of a single very beautiful picture of buildings. The sky above opened up beyond them into the heavens. Through white clouds drawn on a pale yellow canvas, I could glimpse the pale blue heavens beyond, made up of painted tiles like a mosaic. I felt very privileged and happy to see how high the sky rose above my head and the message for me was, "the sky is the limit!"

More recently I had a dream about an old-fashioned coat stand, which had its home in the hallway of my father's house. Again, it was a single picture of clothes draped carelessly over an elegant rise of curved ebony staves. I wrote down what I remembered of the picture, recalling as much detail as possible. Reading through what I had written several times over a period of days, I understood that I was being invited to surrender my old habits ("habit" being an old word for clothes) and let go of my hang-ups.

I invite you to write down your visualizations, dreams and meditative outcomes. Over the years they are a most valuable source of insight and encouragement.

I AM, THEREFORE I CHOOSE

When I, using a little courage, decide to make a positive shift and dip a toe in the waters of change, I notice corresponding movement rippling around me.

Accepting that *I can take charge* of the ways I think and behave turns me into a creator of my own happiness. An initiator is a powerful person who doesn't just wait around for things to happen, but who enjoys harnessing their personal power to carry forward an intention to create a life based around what s/he desires.

Creative Power is a force to be reckoned with: we might like to take some care over how we use it. Every single choice or decision we make carries either a negative or positive charge which has a corresponding impact all around us: we are never in a place where we are not choosing and thereby creating. Descartes would have been more accurate if he had said, "I am, therefore I choose." (7)

There are many millions of people in the world who do not have enough to eat, who have no fresh water to drink, no clean clothes to wear and who endure lives of grinding poverty. For those condemned to living in such wretchedness, the exhortation that we are free to create a different reality for ourselves sounds hollow and unkind, a jeering simplicity that makes light of abject suffering. Yet the outrage that so many endure lives of struggle devoid of opportunity can sting those of us who have more choices into taking action. We in the obscenely affluent "developed world" can make a tangible difference in respecting the aspirations of our world's disadvantaged citizens.

All change starts here with me. If I can locate an ounce of courage to swap the dreary record that is my usual background music for something more upbeat; if I accept myself as a powerful person who selects from among all the thoughts on offer only those which support my happiness, then I have lit the long taper that leads to explosive fulfilment. Does anyone seriously contend that such power is worthless?

I have a constant supply of energy within me, which I can choose to use negatively, passively or positively. That is the big secret of change. While others have forgotten their power, we can remember ours and use our energy and strength to propel us positively along paths we choose. This process gives us a big advantage over those who are simply drifting – and anyone who continually holds up their progress by insisting on their supposed failures, uselessness, guilt, hopelessness, pain, sorrow, powerlessness and so on.

Bad feelings, negativity and bad moods give off dark, heavy vibrations, which clog up our "wish lists" so that anything we might yearn for becomes more difficult to attract. Have you ever noticed how bad feelings can hang around for ages after an argument? Well, that's one reason why. So if I want to reach for something good – or get away from something less than good – I deliberately raise my vibration, getting happy any way I can.

For this, I choose anything that "flicks the switch" to a higher vibe: relaxing, breathing away stress, singing, smiling, repeating "I forgive", laughing, dancing. How would you like to feel? Just feel it. When I remember to clean up my act regularly, awkward situations that might become difficult miraculously evaporate. Choosing what we desire and consciously letting go of what we do not want to keep, is a wonderful way to clear out our emotional closets. Thus, we make room for pleasing experiences.

The process of manifesting works very fast for me when it takes on a double or even a triple aspect. In any situation, FIRST I choose whatever I would prefer to do, have or be; SECOND I consciously release all my fear / sadness / pain / uncertainty / tiredness / loss of courage around the situation, doing my utmost to feel optimistic; then THIRD I might decide to relax with my choice, "because I know that I am safe and guided."

An example might be, "I choose to move house; AND I release all my worries about this exciting choice BECAUSE I know that everything I need comes to me at exactly the right time." Or, "I release my impatience AND I choose to be calm BECAUSE I know that divine timing is perfect and for my benefit." Again, we might say, "I choose to trust that this situation is unfolding for my perfect happiness. Therefore I release all my worries, since I know that I am totally understood and answered completely."

This formula helps us also to clarify our intentions so that we choose more deliberately. It is a pleasure to release our worries, questions and tiredness. We become accustomed to making decisions and statements that feel increasingly refreshing, relaxing and confident. As we end on a positive, nurturing statement, the Universe goes to work on our behalf. It becomes ever easier to voice our preferences routinely and confidently. Thus, we feel purposeful again, energized and ready to take on the next mountain, one small step at a time.

POWER CHOOSES
TO CREATE

In the beginning, according to some, there was Nothing or Everything or God who shared his space with the Man on the Moon. From this Nothing or Everything, "God" or Life has somehow created our World, perhaps with a "Big Bang" that put in place the workings of space, relativity and time. S/he has placed us on Earth and given us tools, our insight, intelligence and freedom to create according to our passions.

I enjoy working with an understanding that, whatever our faith perspective, in the beginning was Life or Source; and Source created all life. From the original whole, Source created all living creatures in all kinds and forms, in all places and spaces, in order for them to experience living and being themselves. From the fact of being part of creation, it would follow that nothing living on Earth needs to justify its being here, by *doing* anything.

However, if we want to do more than just be, of

course we can. One of the strongest urges in the natural world, if not the strongest, is for creation and re-creation. Every life form – birds, bees, all of us, the Universe and everything within it – ultimately exists to mimic its creator, by creating something of and by itself. All life's creatures desire to create and to experience feelings of joy and satisfaction around their personal creative power. Even creatures who die after they have reproduced cannot switch off their desire to make copies of themselves.

Creativity in its wider sense invites us to use our creative powers to express our brightest, best versions of ourselves: to be the best that we can be, right now. Within our artistic and creative talents – which we all have – lie our unique paths to life seen from a lighter, more fulfilling perspective. As naturally as water flowing downhill, we create from the many options that are before us: the good, the bad, the indifferent, the annoying…

Human creativity encompasses everything from expressing pleasure, choosing to be joyful or baking a cake to reinventing the wheel, flying to the moon, singing while we work and motoring off on a weekend away. Whatever we are doing, we can all say together, in our pleasure and enthusiasm, "God, that feels good!" and Life rejoices with us.

When we notice our creative strength, we can agree, "If I am creative, all my thoughts are creative.

All my ideas and beliefs are creative. Hey! I am POWERFUL." We cannot stifle our creative urges permanently. Even sitting still, we are creating *something* with our thoughts and our beliefs. Our beliefs find expression and our passions find outlets, however hard we may push them away or cull them back out of sight.

Time is a framework within which we see our choices playing out. Instead of drifting aimlessly or blaming others by holding them responsible for where we find ourselves, we can take our next small steps deliberately and while we are doing that, declare with a grin, "I prefer to choose and create wisely and joyfully, to make my life meaningful and joyful." Creative energies play around us continuously.

For the most part, we don't realise we are standing right at the centre of our creative power. Since we can't see energy or our thoughts moving, we remain blissfully ignorant of our strength, of the power contained in our thoughts, feelings and desires. Nor do we often listen to guidance which would help us to make wiser choices. But that too, is our choice. We can and often do, choose to ignore help that our intuition sends us – I have been very good at that, for many years.

Stubbornly refusing to listen to all the hints and nudges I have been blessed to receive over the years has hurt me. Because I was in pain, others were hurt too, by my blank refusal to listen or take the gentler path that would have lightened my life and in passing, brightened the lives of others. I have been slow to understand that guidance is sent to each of us with no hint of ego or any hidden agenda, but only with love and solely to make our lives, and the lives of those we love, easier and more enjoyable. Since I have begun to accept this, I want to get on and do what I came here to do, not waste any more time and effort chasing along the most tortuous paths to nowhere or spinning round in circles.

As we move through Life we affect all of its outcomes with our energy, attitudes and preferences. One challenge of living in our heavy atmosphere is to remember that we are not as heavy as we think we are. Although the weighted atmosphere of our planet has its uses and is immensely valuable as a testing ground for our choices, we become lighter as we recall that energy is working in and around us constantly. To recall the light at our core is to realise that we are never alone or isolated. The light within us is the same light that links Source with all its creatures.

We usually catch only rare glimpses of the bigger picture, in coincidences and amusing things that happen everywhere. Since we cannot soar above ourselves and collect up all the threads of meaning into our hands, it helps us feel better if we resist the urge to worry and instead, go all out to cultivate deliberate cheerfulness about what anything means. If we could rise up, we would see the dance of Life moving and understand more clearly our place within it. Seeing ourselves in the dance, our power to move and flex and change would become so much clearer. We would notice the sheer beauty of our deeper feelings and thoughts and delight to express them.

AN AGREEABLE LIFE

In the bigger picture, where we each play a vital part, the Universe reveals itself as essentially non-judgmental. If the Universe carried opinions around and judged everyone, there would be little point in us having any choices. Neither would there be much for us to do. Yet every day, whatever happens to me is the net result of all my choices: what I eat and wear, how I get to work, what I do for a living, the people I am friendly with and where I live, whether I marry, whom I marry, whether to have children; an endless array of choices unfolds for me to select from.

As a species we are gifted with intelligence, intuition, language and strength, as well as the powers of empathy, understanding and faith. We choose when and how we deploy our talents. We choose what we think, what we say and do. Our choices then play out through universal laws such as free will and cause and effect; and in none of this does the Universe pass any judgment.

Whatever I am declaring, in the way I live, the

feelings I have, the thoughts I harbour and whatever I say, *the Universe always agrees with me.* For example, the more earnestly I think, feel and declare that I "want" something, the more I will experience genuine feelings of want. "Want" is an old word for "lack", which means "don't have". If I dwell on my lack or misfortune or even worse, proclaim it in everything I feel, say and do, then *nothing* and *bad luck* are what I experience. When I say, "I want a wonderful life" I am declaring to the whole world and my creative self that my life is not working well for me. So then my subconscious, my good friend who always agrees with me, is constantly casting around for examples that demonstrate the truth of whatever I happen to say, think or believe. The evidence for whatever I declare is missing in my life seems to crowd around me, with some "bad luck" thrown in, just to prove me right. Hey presto! I see problems everywhere and my beliefs are vindicated.

However, regardless of whether our thoughts are good or not so good, this process is always consistent. So, knowing what you don't like about your life, you can probably think of what you would prefer, which in itself begins a process of betterment. It is good to know what we yearn for; but more helpful if we can turn that yearning into the expression of something positive for ourselves. We cannot yearn our way to a beneficial change in our fortunes, since yearning comes from a deep well of lack, loss, sorrow and pain; and yearning implies that we are stuck and cannot move forward.

For a change, we can say, "I am richly rewarded in this life, I am free and full of joy…!" and immediately we begin to notice how this is true for us, in this moment. Our subconscious will help us, by showing us examples of what we declare to be true about ourselves.

What will our problems teach us? "I'm rich!" shouts a man, clutching a five pound note. "I'm poor!" yells his neighbour, scrabbling in his pockets for twenty pounds in loose change. Both statements will prove true. Our power to choose gives us exactly what we feel we are now and exactly what we believe. Therefore, in seeking to benefit fully from my own creative power, it serves me very well when I deliberately notice and accept that I *do* have a wonderful life: a good job, friendly neighbours, a loving partner and deeply fulfilling hobbies. I say, until I believe it: "I love what I have…" or "I have such wonderful friends, family, clothes, neighbours, opportunities and joys." With this cheerful perspective, I generate more positive energy and my life feels much better. When I am generating positive energy, everyone around me benefits too. It is not selfish to be happy, since our happiness gives off great swathes of joy which everyone can share. Our light lights up other people.

The power of our choices operates on at least three different levels: we make deliberate, independent, conscious choices; we can also do what we have always done and make an unconscious choice; and we often do what everyone else is doing, going along with the collective choice, though in doing this, we are ultimately surrendering our power to others. If I am unlucky I may end up being badly affected by choices others have made. These outcomes may not be what I wish for at all, but since I haven't been making many conscious choices of my own, what "happens to me" may be what I end up with by default. Sometimes we even make a deliberate choice not to choose, in which case it is easy to see how we may collect the impact from choices that other people are making.

Our personal and collective choices have an impact far greater than we realise. Multiplied by many millions, our less thoughtful and negative behaviours reverberate around the planet, causing suffering and loss to untold numbers of others who don't participate in what we choose and whom we never intended to harm. Believe it or not, our species' collective actions are that powerful.

Very often, we forget our power. I used to balance uncomfortably on the edges of other people's lives, doing what they asked and working to please them. What I would have preferred to do hardly entered the equation and life was driving me crazy, until I realised that the way to change was to take control.

How easily we understand the word "creative" when it is applied to activities like singing, dancing, drawing and painting. We always keep our capacity to make other, deeper choices. For example, would you rather be a "poor, trapped home-maker with no income and no job prospects" or "a loving partner and parent who looks after the family and cherishes the freedom to be independent"? Objectively, both sets of circumstances are the same. It is how we see ourselves that makes all the difference. Whatever I am articulating – whatever I think, feel, do or say – I am creating. With every thought of joy, I create my delight.

JOY IS ENERGY

Do you play games? Do you laugh? When did you last go to a party where you had real fun? Not the kind where everyone stands around gossiping meaninglessly and drinking too much alcohol to fend off boredom. When did you last look about you and say, *I'm having a great time, I feel really wonderful…this is a great day.* When did you last ache with laughter?

Perhaps as you read this paragraph, you let out a wistful sigh and think "Gosh, it has been ages. There was that time…in Italy on holiday…God, was it really TWELVE years ago?" Maybe you feel impatient with my questions: "I don't have time for all that stuff now, for goodness' sake. My husband has Alzheimer's, my kids hardly talk to each other and only visit me when they are broke or have nothing better to do. It has been a while since I really laughed, of course, but that doesn't mean I'm unhappy!" Privately, you may then take a few seconds to work out that the last time you remember jumping for joy was at college, maybe fifteen years ago. Don't worry, that doesn't have to be a problem. Happiness and enthusiasm can even be faked: if you are miserable, jump up and down and say "I feel great!" Fake it till you make it. Start now. Do not wait until you have finished reading. Have a smile break.

Do you have a young child or do you work with young children? Are they forever playing games? Do they laugh and talk constantly and ask unusual questions, always inventing new jokes and amusements? The natural state of young children is to play games *all the time* if we let them. It is through playing that children learn how the world works. Why should we be any different?

The most wonderful things we often recall about children are the small moments when they pulled us away from our "have to" lives and made us laugh. Laughter is good, happy and freeing and we can all bring to mind the small moments of joy children offer us long after the "must do" things are gone.

Although children are born brimming over with love, almost as soon as they leave the womb we adults seem to be working out how to make them "good" or "well behaved". It seems to me that many adults are engaged in various well-meaning attempts to get children to "do what they are told" (all the boring, unimaginative stuff) and "grow up", whatever that means. Privately, I have long nursed a conviction that adults are engaged in a programme to turn multi-coloured and multi-dimensional little people into black-and–white copies of themselves, bored and desperate much of the time.

The good news is that, for many of us, reclaiming our joy is simple, if we can learn to laugh and play again. When we laugh, all the things we *think* are important dissolve and we see a world that is new, different, fresh and exciting. Laughter and joy shatter all our old ideas, most of which are probably out of date anyway. We can replace fusty memories and our notions of "good" behaviour with some invigorating, wonderful inspiration, beautiful colourful dreams based firmly around what we enjoy; what makes us laugh, sing, dance, tell jokes and generally behave like a little child.

We surely do not want to turn children into mere copies of ourselves, do we? Do they not deserve a fresh chance to be themselves? And, if you retort that children have to learn about the hard realities of life, I would answer that it is adults in their seriousness who have made life a hardship, carelessly casting aside the inborn ease of it. Have we looked at the shape our world is in? If this is "how the world works" then all I can say is, it won't be working much longer. We'd better shake up and start dancing.

YOUR PASSIONS
FUEL YOUR JOY

Do you cherish a deep, grand dream? Or harbour a whole fistful of ambitions in your heart? How does *passion* feel for you? Does *passion* conjure up visions of men gesticulating wildly in the midst of a heated discussion? A lady who dances a lot and likes to sing at the top of her voice? Whatever you imagine, there is sure to be lots of movement and feeling. That is great! Movement and feeling are two impulses which shake us away from the dead things we do because we become convinced we have no choice. Moving and feeling are fantastic keys to change. And the freedom and delight which we can unearth from making honest choices are what we came here to discover.

It can be a real challenge unearthing our passions. We spend many years being educated apart from our unique impulses; and in the process we shed many small, seemingly insignificant, pleasures.

Do we do things not because we feel drawn to them by passion, but because we think we "ought" to or because everyone else is doing them too and saying that we "should"? Instead of allowing our passions to inform our choices, instead of taking opportunities to learn how to craft a life for ourselves based around our joys, we play safe with our selections, our careers, perhaps quietly seduced by status, the prospect of money or security in later life. Many of us choose what we do in the belief that the most important goals of learning are to be "rich", "respectable" or "responsible" or even to know and mingle with the right crowd. But if we achieve these objectives, once we land the prestigious job with the fat cheque, find the big house, the beautiful helpmate, often we feel there is something missing. The large space, the clean, elegant living, can be cold and lonely unless we make room for our creative desires.

I would love to be in a household setup in which I got to make the mess and someone else would tidy up. Most of the time, I automatically do the cooking, clearing, washing and the wiping down, even though I hate household chores. But here's the thing – no-one is forcing me to do any of it. My husband does not stand behind me making veiled references about the state of the kitchen and he has never, ever suggested that "the carpets could do with a clean, darling". Not once has he hinted that I might make his dinner or press his shirts. So, he is really an ideal husband, who will no doubt be delighted to see me writing this evening, well into "supper hour" when I would ordinarily be cooking something delicious and nutritious. Maybe, when he arrives home we can cook up something between us. That would be fun. We can chat, share and work together.

It is a sad reflection that growing up and growing older seem to involve an almost total suppression of those impulses and pleasures which make us uniquely happy. Our happiness, after all, gives us our energy for life. What do we imagine our imagination is for? Does life gift us our talents so that we simply shut them out? Or can we take our courage in both hands and embrace our creative abilities, allowing them to energize our lives?

I am not suggesting that we should all give up lucrative jobs to go and live on an ashram. To rediscover the meaning in our lives it is *not* necessary to trek to the Himalayas or travel deep into the Amazon jungle. We can simply rediscover what makes us passionate. The definition of "fulfilled" includes "achieving one's potential or desire" (8). The deeper a desire is buried, the further we dig to recover it. Have you ever tried breaking up concrete? You need a power drill and strong arms – with a little courage and faith thrown in.I encourage you to shrug off any hard casing of cynicism, boredom or the weight of expectation that you may be carrying around. That kind of baggage is surplus to requirements, as we discover while we are doing this work to free ourselves. It is *very okay* to leave rigid routines behind. To live happily in this life we can use every tiny scrap of positive, happy energy we can lay our hands on: our passions answer some of life's most challenging questions.

Our reinvention begins when we unlock those parts of us which are rusty or numb from lack of use. Intangible gifts we have forgotten or ignored for too long, like dreaming, the ability to do nothing and firing up our imagination are important. They deserve to be brought out of the closet and respected. Unused, our talents wither away, while we ask ourselves, "Why is life so boring…?"

I love drawing chalky, messy pictures. I also like singing and composing songs, reading and writing. There was a time when I became used to thinking, "Oh goodness, I am feeling bored with drawing this picture, but this is something I am supposed to enjoy; so maybe I am no good at this, after all" and I would give up, again. Thoughts like these were a repeating, frustrating habit. I believed that, because I got "switched off" or tired, I lacked perseverance and talent; and that therefore my pleasures were worthless. The feeling that something was "not worth" persisting with became endemic and my life was littered with half-baked ideas and half-finished projects. Held in the grip of that mentality, it became ever harder for me to surrender to the urge to paint, draw or write whenever it popped up its head. The same lack of persistence was evident in many other parts of my life.

As the years pass, I see that I can indeed do all these things I enjoy, as well as many others, though I probably handle each one better at different times. It appears that my desires rotate – how cool is that? Nowadays I can choose to see whatever I am doing as a bit of fun, light and dark, serious or whimsical. If any one idea loses momentum, I can try another or venture off into something completely different. Increasingly, I find I stick with half-finished projects, leave them awhile and return to them again later, taking each one forward by small, inching steps. I am discovering delightful patience for creations that may be less than perfect, which makes it much easier to pick up an unfinished project the next time I get the urge. Willing to devote fresh energy and time I can more easily take it up to the next level or to completeness: how satisfying! Better still, I also learn the beauty of doing something on a whim, because doing it simply makes me feel good.

So, have fun! If you have forgotten what fun is, look for something that makes your toes tingle: experiment. It can be something very simple and it doesn't need to cost anything. Go to the beach and listen to the waves. Pick up a bagful of litter from your local beauty spot and recycle as much of it as you can. Walk by a river and watch for the birds. Take off for a long hike in the hills. Visit friends. Take up invitations to go to concerts and galleries. Eat a lovely meal and take your time. Clear out your wardrobe; give the stuff you secretly despise to charity and wear your best outfit on an "ordinary" day. Do something for the sake of it. If you find joy, you will not be fearful. If you stop to consider, you will remember that it is impossible to be truly happy and fearful at the same time.

If, having invested courage and optimism to dig through the sediment of the past, you uncover old passions or discover new ones, hold onto them. Cherish them! The small and great things we find to amuse us make a difference and if something thrills you, it is important.

Often we know what we desire but we find it challenging to go one tiny step further and follow through on our preferences. Honouring our choices is a very powerful way to align our hopes and allow our lives to flow forward as we would like them to, rather than being shunted about by other people's expectations. We all nurture dreams, of winning a million pounds, setting up our own businesses, making it into the major leagues or escaping the rat race…and expressing a simple choice – *what would I like to do now?* – is at the heart of every grand ambition. Even so, we don't need to quit our jobs or move house, we don't need to upset the apple cart with grand gestures (unless they are the outcome of twenty-five years of yearning and hoping and dreaming, in which case, now might be a good time). Making our own decisions feels refreshing. The result may only be a small shift in our centre of gravity, but even that starts something new.

You do not need to think or worry too much about how an enthusiasm can possibly be "made to fit" into your "ordinary" life. Please, having found something which buoys you up, resist the temptation to *think* your cherished inspiration to death. Inspiration comes from a light space that we do not recognise with our brains. Perhaps that is why we often treat inspiration with suspicion. Yet, if we keep returning to the germ of an idea with acceptance and faith, answers come to us, step by step, attracted by our intention and our desire. Passions grow naturally from within.

Say you work at the minimum wage and you have a wife and two young children to support. What is it you dream of doing? What makes you grin and want to laugh aloud? Maybe you would enjoy making sculptures of junk, but there is no space for them in your home. It is tempting then, to dismiss the whole idea, isn't it? Conventional wisdom tells us that following this passion would be hugely impractical and a waste of time. Where would you put all your stuff? Your wife and family expect something more grown up from you. Why bother?

In hoping to match up life as I currently live it, with a desire that goes off, perhaps, in the opposite direction, it is sometimes helpful if the leap between my dreams and what am doing at the moment is not *so* great that my heart gives up at the first hurdle. If you dream of being a sculptor working in Milan, it is probably going to be hard to bring that dream to fruition if you imagine you will be "discovered" by a famous artist who happens to spot one of your pieces, especially if you work in the basement of a call-centre in Leeds and never make anything artistic.

As a start, imagine your dream in all its delicious details so that you see small, perhaps even tiny, practical steps filling in some of the gaps on the way to your dream. To play with this example further, you might see yourself looking for pieces of beautiful junk in the area's reclamation yards at weekends. Making a day of it, you could take your children along and let them choose with you. Or you might take an empty yogurt pot and turn it into something beautiful, collect a few interesting pebbles from a nearby beach, paint pictures on bits of wood or look around for community classes in experimental art. You might get together with a friend and sketch out ideas or browse a local library. When you think and talk about your ambition, you may notice adverts in the paper for exhibitions. Your friends and strangers you meet may offer suggestions that you would never have thought of. Once we engage with an idea, other helpful thoughts come to us and we see things we would not have noticed before, which act as pointers to our next steps.

If you still can't see where your delight might fit into your life and are tempted to give it all up as too much hard work, agree that personal delight is a form of truth, reminding us of what makes us unique. Our brains make good tools for analysing things and for working out ideas. While it is true that we like to "get our head around things", have you ever noticed how the job of understanding every last detail ends up sucking out the juicy bits, leaving behind a feeling like cold leftovers? It is often the "thinking" about an idea which kills it stone dead. If we have come this far, which is a long way, it is a short step to accepting that all we need do next is give our dreams permission and space to flower of their own accord. Life has a gentle style of moving us forward down avenues we least expect. So, let life help you and don't try to see all the ways.

I was thinking about setting down some songs that I had written. With no idea where to start, I would have liked an opinion on what I had sung into a hand-held Dictaphone. My desire and my Dictaphone were all I had and the whole idea of taking this flight of fancy any further was scary, somehow. I looked at a couple of websites and the local phone directory for ideas of what recording facilities might be available locally. Later that week, I was sitting in the car waiting to turn into the main road. Directly in front of us was a van with the logo and phone number of a local recording studio printed all over it. I would not have noticed that if I had not been thinking about it. Still, I was surprised. How often is a van from an out-of-town music studio going to be sitting directly in front of me?

We tend to find what we are looking for. If we ask for help, ideas can be put our way, especially when we resist saying, "I don't believe it, this is just incredible!" when something wonderful does happen. So take time to discover what makes you really laugh and your tummy flutter and go looking for it.

TAKING LIFE FOR GRANTED

We take it for granted that what we feel like just now, feels right. If we are used to thinking in a certain way, for example if we tend to worry or suffer with depression or anxiety, our mind will have been very accommodating through the years. What is more, the longer we have such feelings, the harder it can be to visualize any life without them and the longer it takes to establish different patterns of being. We may even miss our old ways, however unhappy they made us.

To ease the process of our re-invention, I find it extremely reassuring to remind myself of two things. Firstly, when we experiment with more positive ways of thinking and feeling, our lives may indeed improve markedly for a while, before sliding back to worse again. Oh, great! That doesn't sound encouraging, does it? Don't worry! I am being honest so that you don't think that you have missed the turn-off on the road somewhere.

For example, I may be making a point of thinking new, good, positive thoughts about my home life, such as, "My family life is peaceful and joyful. We are all very happy". For a while, everything feels and moves wonderfully. "This really works!" I mutter incredulously and it does, it really feels hopeful and sparkly and filled with new energy. Then, wham! Before I know it, my husband and I are having a blazing row. How did that happen?

Perhaps I am sincerely visualizing ease and lack of stress in my life and after a bit of "beginner's luck" I carelessly lock myself out of my flat; or I am inviting prosperity to come stay and after picking coins off the carpet and saving on fares, I lose my purse. Setbacks like these are very common.

Quick as a flash I am tempted to think, "Well, I might as well go back to the way I used to be, at least I knew what to expect and I didn't do stupid things like locking myself out of my flat in my dressing-gown! What an overgrown idiot I am." Before I realise what has happened, I am back in my old groove...

Before giving up your hopes for wonderful change as a waste of time, remember: *slipping back is normal*. Encountering reversals does not mean we have failed or that changing our ways of thinking is a waste of time. If you are driving in a strange town and lose your way, do you get angry or do you turn around and try again?

Talk gently with yourself and try to see the funny side. If we have the presence of mind to stand back and *observe* what happens, we might notice that the strength of a reversal, the time it takes for life to perk up again, serves us by revealing how ingrained our oldest habits are. The longer we have held attitudes, the harder they fight to stay when we are trying to let them go. They fight and then they fight some more.

I could not believe that this happened to me recently. After years of working on brightening my perspective, I was coming to a point when everything was making sense. I was confidently asserting, "I really am very happy!" and indeed I truly was. Singing, I went to say goodnight to Seline in her darkened room and suddenly I tripped and fell. I crashed into her chest of drawers, banging my hip and breaking the bottom drawer of a very substantial piece of furniture. The poor girl was trying to get to sleep as I sat there on the floor of her bedroom in a daze of disbelief, frantically gluing the drawer back together. Even suspecting that this was down to resistance could not console me at the time.

I was wondering how to get past this latest reversal. It would have been very easy to sigh, hold up my hands and say, "See how hard I try? And *nothing ever changes for me.* I think I will just give up, it is all too hard. How did I think I could change the attitudes of a lifetime? Life is just a hard, shitty slog and I have the bruises to prove it."

There are several passive aspects to my personality which just accept what happens, because to make a fuss feels like too much hard work and rather pointless: what can I do, after all, about having been born disabled? The weight of all that passivity was, yet again, threatening to drown my latest hopes for a more up-beat attitude. Then I remembered my inner Hag. She is very vocal, a strident and strong part of my personality, one of the very few aspects that, since my childhood has had the courage to say what she thinks. In her own angry and upsetting way, she has done her best to defend me through the years. The Hag has been very useful, acting as a counterweight to save me from sinking into sorrow and never coming out again. Suddenly I recognised that I might use her determination to help me. So long as I move her away from hostility, her raw energy is put to better use and her role in my life is helpfully redefined. Immediately, the Hag becomes my new friend, a powerful, strong woman who has learned from her experiences and who refuses to be deflected from her choices. Her strength is within me. Now I keep on deploying a prescription of positive beliefs, knowing that she is happy to help me complete the course. In time, the anger of her energy becomes muted and turns towards acceptance, so that some days I find myself merely accepting what is happening, without any strong reaction.

Scientists might explain that if my subconscious has understood life as a struggle, then even when I am consciously trying to establish a new, easier way, my subconscious takes its own sweet time to catch up with the "new me". Our conscious and subconscious minds like to run along together, like best friends on the jogging track. To any changes, the subconscious will first respond by saying, "Hey, I don't recognise this new behaviour, how about some of the old? Old feels familiar! New feels uncomfortable!" In my experience it makes no difference that we may be trying to feel better, more secure, more at peace. Our deeper reaction is always the same: anything unfamiliar is dangerous. To ward off danger, our old pal, brother habit, does his utmost to set up a situation which feels more familiar to the good old, bad old days.

Learning new attitudes is exactly like other forms of learning. It requires patience and perseverance in the study of new skills and attitudes which we hope to acquire. *There is always a time lapse* and there are bound to be reversals. Recognition is the key. It takes a while for the subconscious to recognise the new you. Eventually the truth dawns that any changes which make us feel happier are not threatening, but very helpful indeed and great fun. Therefore, keep looking at where you hope to go and seeing yourself where you aim to be.

If like me, you enjoy pictures and puns, imagine that all your thoughts are contained in a large pot, full to the brim. If you nudged the pot with your foot, its contents would slop all over your shoe…If we are trying to change our thoughts, to alter the mix, where are all our new insights going to fit? Inevitably, some of the old, dirty stuff has to go *somewhere* to make room for the new and that "somewhere" is usually out into the open, all over our shiny new thoughts.

When I am *making real progress* I often find that, for a time, all goes well. Then – splat! – When I am not thinking about it, I slip on some old messy mind stuff that I have carelessly left lying around. I run down a familiar groove and get stuck there for a while. Rather than feel that I have a split personality, I ask, "Is this resistance?" We all slip from time to time. When I need encouragement, I say, "This is just a fearful reaction…it is all resistance. The real me – happy, confident, certain – is moving in the right direction towards the inevitable truth that I am worthy to receive happiness".

The second aspect of our caution is that any change in our attitudes from depressed or negative to happier and more positive, feels light and wonderful. Suddenly we find we have more energy, we laugh more easily and problems do not bother us as much as they used to.

Then, suddenly, Wham! Out of the blue, occasionally very quickly, we may feel emotional, deeply angry, depressed or physically sick. Mood changes and ailments descend as if from nowhere out of a clear blue sky, making us feel vulnerable, as if we are being swung about on the end of a rope without a foothold. When this happens it feels very disconcerting and challenges our whole perception of being in control.

I reconcile myself to strange mood swings and changes in my physical health by remembering that when anyone has been depressed for twenty years, this is a stable, though negative, condition which the mind and body have adjusted to and learned to tolerate, however gnarled and withered the outcome: we may be grinding along in first gear, but it is a stable place to be and we "know" what to expect, which is generally not very much. We grow accustomed to a certain level of physical, mental and emotional discomfort and we may even resent or fear feeling different, as if, in the absence of certain pre-occupations, there is something missing in our lives.

When we move up a couple of gears we usually need time to adjust, re-tuning our minds and bodies to work at a higher, more positive frequency. For example, whenever I am moving through a major breakthrough aimed at ditching a negative habit or belief, I seem to get a head cold. While it is foolish of me to abandon my scarf before the end of February, I also see that my subconscious is *unfamiliar* with my happiness and tries to re-connect to what it recognises. Head, heart and body are all connected. Given time, physical symptoms lessen, as our head, heart and body sing together from the new, happier song sheet.

So until positive shoots of joy take root and bloom, please be patient, gentle and kind to yourself. Forgive your lapses in judgment and behaviour. Instead, learn to applaud your efforts. Enduring change happens slowly and gently. If someone had reassured me in the early days, "Just keep going with the good stuff until your body, your brain and your beliefs catch up with you," I would have felt a lot happier.

Go easy on yourself. Even if you have ruined your mother's best antique tablecloth, locked yourself out of the house, got lost driving around a conurbation or missed the plane – is that the end of the world? When you are being hard on yourself, just imagine that, standing tearfully in front of you, feet turned in sadly, shoes all scuffed and dirty, is someone you love, who has done all these things and worse. What would you do? You would probably put your arms around them and ponder the hundred-and-one things you might say to cheer them up. Or wait peacefully until they have stopped crying and then offer a handkerchief and a joke to make them smile. Gentleness makes you feel better and improves the outcome for everyone.

Our spirits, minds and bodies all have purposes which blend together in ways we are just beginning to appreciate. When we feel happy, our physical health improves. When we eat well, our mental health improves. When we sleep well and do things we enjoy, our spiritual health improves. When our different aspects are cared for, we connect more quickly with our best reason for being here: to be as happy as we can be.

In the midst of a daily moan, I stop myself in my tracks by thinking of the whole process of change as a straightforward "junk thoughts" detoxification program. I find the comparison with junk food very helpful, since the same roller-coaster ride can happen when we have a junk food detox and we tend to be less hard on ourselves when wondering whether we really need that extra packet of crisps. Just as I don't wish to eat popcorn for breakfast or drink sugary tea, I feel happier when I stop blaming other people for my situation, manipulating them into feeling sorry for me or cowering fearfully when the next credit card bill is due, because *I feel stronger when I do something positive instead.*

OPPORTUNITY KNOCKS

Working alone most of the day can become isolating and repetitive. So, one day I may decide that my life needs to become more exciting and interesting. Instead of feeling trapped by what I do every day, one antidote is to remind myself, "I have a really exciting life and many opportunities come to me". In reply, life immediately starts sending me excitement. The phone rings, invitations arrive in the post, neighbours knock at the door, I make friends when I go swimming. Because I reset my head space to "optimistic", life feels brighter and more fun.

Even so, I am constantly surprised by the number of times in a day I cut myself off from wonderful experiences. The "slammed door" is a common example. I turn away a pleasing suggestion with a refusal, "I'm sorry, I can't," or, "Not just now". Do you do this too? If "No, thanks!" is our automatic response to most invitations, how can goodness come into our lives? I also short-circuit my freedom with my private list of one hundred other things I "should" be doing now: "I have to go and make the dinner or I will be late for my meeting". There are times when I may even be quite hostile, saying things like, "Don't be an idiot, of course you can't have a nap in the afternoon (or sex?), whoever heard of such a thing! Degenerate!"

We all desire peace, freedom, ease and relaxation, don't we? If a suggestion fills us with a relieved smile, we can pause for a moment and experiment with replying, "Yes, that would be good. How about now…?" If an idea makes you want to dance, go for it. As for sex in the afternoon…

There are other ways we shut out the good. I always secretly thought swimming was rather dull and predictable; and when I went to the pool, I counted lengths. Not long ago someone said, "Well, I never count lengths, I just enjoy swimming and when I've had enough, I get out." My first thought was, "what a waste" but then I realised he was right: counting lengths is a total chore. When I get to around about fourteen, I always forget what number I am at; and, although I most enjoy the relaxed peacefulness that comes from swimming, I have always clung grimly to a number, as if it was the answer to my prayers. Now *that's* dull, isn't it? So I've taken that advice and simply enjoy swimming now.

Without meaning to, we can get strapped to the wheels of some bad habits, big and small, which might just keep rolling into infinity, unless we have the presence of mind to notice them and decide to stop them. We then think that a bad situation is inevitable instead of noticing our part in keeping it rolling. Here is a scenario that reminds me of what life felt like for me a few years ago.

Suppose I am in a bad mood with my husband one morning, because I suspect he has forgotten that today is our wedding anniversary. I strop around the house being silent or sarcastic but without once hinting, "Darling, do you know what day it is today?" I could come right out and remind him gently, "It's our wedding anniversary, why don't we go out for a meal this evening? I would really like that." Instead, I decide that he is psychic and in the middle of his early morning preparations for work, he is supposed to guess that I am upset and what is bothering me. He doesn't, indeed he hardly notices I am annoyed, which is another black mark against him. I get crosser until finally I explode and end a tirade of abuse with, "Of course you should have remembered – you would have, if you loved me!"

Perhaps the poor man looks up, starts to fidget and leaves for work in a hurry. In that case I am left alone, probably with a host of jobs to do, but I feel bad with him and myself. I fume, cry, wipe up and get on and then I feel guilty for what I said. "I am a stupid woman, for all my nonsense." Maybe I phone and apologise. "Okay, darling, I'm really sorry…" and still feel a total fool. I am also worried: it is very possible that my husband won't be as forgiving next time.

So I think I should cook up a lovely meal, to show how sorry I am, even though I hate cooking and this just adds to the burdens of the day. Inevitably I get cross again, because I don't actually want to cook. Then he arrives home after I have spent two hours making curry, rice and all the trimmings from scratch and all I hear him asking is, "Where is the salt?" Again I get cross, because he should have noticed how hard I worked and I fume...and so it goes on.

The wheel rolls round and round, except that with each turn of the wheel, the circles we move in – the options open to us – seem to shrink very slightly. We come up with lots of excuses for our behaviour, blaming others, reasoning, "It's all their fault". As our options contract, we may even choose another partner instead of asking ourselves of how we ended up leaving such a wonderful person. Learning nothing from this type of exchange, we repeat our mistakes and may pass many years wondering why our relationships feel unrewarding and difficult.

On the other hand, if I am lucky I may recognise familiar patterns. No matter how inevitable a poor situation feels, no matter how little familiarity I may have with success or positive outcomes; regardless, something has to change *with me* if I am to salvage some joy and pleasure in my life and relationships.

Whatever the rights and wrongs in any circumstance and despite every perceived misfortune, I can always turn my attention towards those results I prefer to see. If I can find enough self-belief to gently or firmly explain what I hope for, given a bit of practice, I get some straight answers and it is refreshing to discover that we can achieve mutual understanding without crushing the opposition.

Honesty makes my life so much easier. Even if the truth is not especially palatable, it is a fresh take on a situation, which everyone can work with. People who live around me hopefully begin to realise with relief that I do actually mean what I say. If, like me, you have been caught up in damaging behaviour for years and suddenly decide to change, you may be sincere and taking great strides forward, but it will probably take a while before your significant others believe the change, recognise your sincerity and trust you again. Don't give up your efforts without allowing your friends time to come alongside the "new you". In the meantime, can you see a happy outcome?

In a sense this idea falls neatly into two halves. First, cutting out bad habits is an excellent start. We can all stop cursing our lives with careless or negative thinking. But for best results, we can also pump in lots of good feelings by lavishing praise, consideration, affection and love on each other.

Another wonderful gift is forgiveness to those who

may have hurt you, *especially yourself*. Having put considerable conscious effort into making changes for happier relationships, you may feel that the real, calm, lovely you is coming out to play at last. If so, feelings of regret may not be far behind. It has taken me decades to tackle my negative behaviour and I wish I'd had more courage to do this when I was younger – so many wasted years! But I also know that there is no virtue in spending the *next* few years wallowing in recriminations, self-pity and regret for lost opportunities. After all, if I had known that what I was doing was making my life unnecessarily difficult, I would not have been doing it. We do many things without thinking, because that is what we have always done and it takes real insight to notice that we now prefer to do things differently; and courage to experiment with new ideas. Think of regrets and sorrow as the heel of a loaf of bread which may well be hard to swallow: we need an extra dollop of jam spread on the hard corners to make them palatable. When we are learning a new, more honest way of being, feelings of sadness may come to remind us of our failures and may even threaten to overwhelm us. Take courage! There is, unfortunately, no better way to learn than by making mistakes. Grieve if you need to; and take comfort from knowing that the past is over. We can let it go.

If we have done something foolish or hurtful and

we would like to make amends, instead of seeing a dreaded confrontation or living with endlessly recycled regrets, now is a great opportunity to make a new choice. We can choose to see the situation working out well, the way we would like it to. When we put positive feelings and beliefs into seeing a great outcome, at the very least we feel a whole lot better.

It's a truism that I recognise *my* faults in the behaviour of others. How else could I recognise them? I can turn around any difficult situation by rephrasing it. Thus, if my daughter is being rude, she must be getting that from someone, probably me. If my husband is being uncommunicative, maybe I could put my book down and converse.

If I want a spontaneous and creative life, I might like to try some spontaneous creating. The quality of my life really does start and end with me.

If we don't like the story of our lives we can *change the script* and see our life unfolding as we desire. Our imagination can take each of us anywhere we desire.

SCRIPTS AND SUBTEXTS

The subtexts of our lives – our subconscious beliefs – contain all those things we think are true about ourselves. For example, we accept that writers spend their days writing; mothers should spend their time being motherly; and an office worker has a duty to turn up to the office and be productive and willing every work day. As well as our "professional" subtexts, we also have personal ones, such as "I should go swimming today" (swimming is good for me), "I should make the most of my free time doing things I have to do" (before the holidays start at the end of the week). "I should go shopping" (we need food). The number of things we should be doing is endless and exhausting: common to all these things is a feeling of obligation.

But what if we now agreed that just this second, at this precise moment, we don't have to accept or listen to any of our subtexts? When we feel heavy, it may be because beliefs like these are weighing us down. So how about we release these old stories and write a different story, starting where we are just now?

I used to fret around the house, telling my family to "hurry up!" when I was impatient to go out. Then the thought occurred that I would be much happier if I focused on getting myself ready. Others would either follow me out the door or not. Nowadays, that principle can be expressed as fixing my intention and then following through with it, regardless of anyone else might be thinking, saying or doing.

First we decide: what are we going to do, have or be? We are always deciding. So, do you crave peace and quiet? Do you yearn to quit your job? Are you really unhappy in your flat or do you want to stay? Would you like to meet more friends or learn how to master a new language? Do you yearn to be happy, whatever you are doing? Be very clear about what you intend. For once in your life, be really selfish until you unearth the truth.

For the purposes of this exercise, don't start thinking about what your partner needs, what your children would prefer or all the other things you have to do. No-one else can fix your decision, your internal compass, for you; and you cannot fix anyone else's. Start by fixing your own; do not clutter your picture by worrying too much about what other people want, expect or need from you. That is for them to decide and you disempower them if you think otherwise.

If you look at *any* situation in which you feel uncomfortable, at its heart you will find a conflict of preferences. Use your feelings to rediscover what you truly desire. Then, fix your intention on your choice or remedy: go eat a lovely meal, take a holiday, leave your abusive partner, look for a new job: work at something interesting for a change; or change the way you work so that your passion is reignited. Leave your desk and rest. What you decide may not be practical to do immediately, but the clarity of your intention makes you feel a million times better and helps the Universe to answer your prayers.

When we respect and follow through on our preferences, our children behave better and our partners may either like it, feel threatened or walk out. If I have been too obliging for too long and I need some space, I might say to my husband, "You can make your own supper this evening, I am going to a movie which starts at six." Of course, having thought about this, I know he will be fine. My daughter usually has a meal at lunch and I may even know that my husband dined today at a restaurant of his choice. "It's my turn for some fun," I say and skip out the door. If your partner loves you, s/he will probably heave a sigh of relief and say, "Thank goodness!"

Consider: The rest of the world will not come unstuck if I decide to follow my dream; but if I ignore my dream – which gets louder and more insistent as time goes on – my world may come unstuck. The reason many people stay in unhappy – that is, conflicted – situations, is that they know what they want, but they refuse to act, worrying that they "should" do this, that or the other thing first or that they "ought" to wait and help others to be happy, to be free, before seeing to their own wishes. Or they wait for someone to rescue them. They sit by the phone or hope for a letter, an invitation. That is not the way to make things happen. If we think, "I want to be happy but I can't be happy until I make you happy too" there is confusion. If you are happy doing what you choose, your positive attitude and happiness inspires others.

Look at the successful people in the world: mothers, workers, businessmen, children who unselfconsciously paddle in the fountain and grin from ear to ear...and ask yourself, what is it that distinguishes them from me? It is the certainty of their intentions and their refusal to deviate. They will not be constantly changing their minds or sabotaging their plans by "just finishing the housework first."

Whenever we want to do something, whether that might be tidying out a drawer, painting a picture, trying out a new recipe or phoning a friend, there is no reason to wait for the perfect day, the right conjunction of the planets, the right moment, the perfect place. Waiting is too often the consolation prize of the fearful and I should know: I sat waiting and hoping for things to be perfect *before* I took that step. Now, let us just be brave and begin. Beginning is not hard, except that I then wish I hadn't wasted so much time waiting for the perfect day, the perfect opportunity… Whenever I quit worrying and just get on out there and do something, I feel refreshed and energized. However slowly, I'm moving in the direction of my dreams.

ASKING FOR HELP

In the daily round, inevitably, we grapple with dilemmas and difficulties, many of which we have to work through alone. We cannot express ourselves powerfully if we constantly look to others for approval, love or permission. If we are fearful of disapproval, we could be waiting a long time – a lifetime! Yet, there will be times when we need support and advice. I know that asking for help looks easy, but stepping outside habits of defiant independence is a lifelong challenge. I have been that woman who would rather have her pubic hair pulled out with tweezers than ask for assistance.

But there are ways to ask which don't involve grovelling. And most people *love* being asked to lend a hand now and then. We can approach a friend who is likely to have encountered the same problem and ask them what they did. One time, I got all upset because I was running late for something. Tearfully I confessed to an experienced mother-of-three that my daughter, then a baby, would not eat her breakfast and she answered, "Well, maybe she just isn't hungry!" and laughed easily. That cheered me up very fast.

I have been in some tricky situations – stuck in a snowdrift, upside down on a subway escalator, lost on a hillside in the rain. I have learned, mostly from seeing people smile when they help me, that it is pointless soldiering on alone. We gain so much from an extra pair of hands and a different point of view. An independent attitude works well if we believe that the world is a hostile place. Then, of course, we are in enemy territory where it pays to be as self-sufficient as possible. But none of the people who have come to my aid could be called unfriendly and several have probably saved my life. One message of this book is that if we choose peaceful thoughts, we usually see the world as a friendly place. It follows that we can easily ask for and, graciously accept, help.

Asking for help goes further. If we have even the faintest belief in god(s), guardian angels, spirit guides or the afterlife, we can ask "them" for help too. I have often read that angels would love to help us and are waiting about in the wings (cute pun!) for just this purpose. I prayed desperately for many years, without conspicuous success. These days I find that offering a sincere request for help with a specific problem brings the best results. I smile to think of all these very beautiful beings hovering hopefully. So, if you feel like it, ask for help. Who knows who may be listening?

I do feel for God sometimes. S/he gets to listen to all the tearful, desperate stuff. I know, because this is what I sent up to the sorting office in the sky for many years. Rarely did I approach my problems cheerfully, with serenity or faith. Then I found this passage: "You pray in your distress and your need: would that you might pray also in the fullness of your joy and in your days of abundance." (9). I began to understand that if I can feel good about what I am praying for, it is easier to come by.

If you want to feel better anywhere, anytime, all you have to do is start where you are standing, lying or sitting. Look at what you have. Think about the beauty of your breathing. Sing a song, dance a little dance (you can even do this in your imagination), paint a picture, think of a beautiful colour, lots of beautiful colours and FEEL THANKFULNESS. If you feel you have nothing to be thankful for, pull in your field of vision so that you find *something* to feel pleased about. You have two good legs and can walk? Well, isn't that fantastic? How about entering the next local marathon and raising money for wheelchair-bound athletes who are planning a foreign holiday? You can talk? Well, how about telephoning your parents? How about telling your partner you love them and appreciate their support? It is up to you. The list is endless.

Cultivating an awareness of appreciative gratitude brings in more of what we are grateful for. If you are looking for success, try getting yourself to a place where you feel successful and then give thanks for your success. In an attitude of appreciative thanks, prayers are powerful. We can also put on our listening hat sometimes. If we spend all our time in earnest, noisy entreaties, how can we hear anything that God or the angels might say? How can S/he get a word in edgeways?

I'VE GOT MY OWN KEYS

We live and breathe and act and do and ponder, often without much thought. Many of our daily activities do not require a great deal of conscious thought. To achieve a surprising range of everyday tasks, it is enough that we do what we have done before, perhaps refining our preferences slowly over time, but, basically, using the knowledge we have already gained to make life quicker and easier. It is an added bonus that we can then do two or even three things at once. In many ways, our minds are designed to do lots of stuff on autopilot, so that we are more efficient. Then also, because of what we have learned to do automatically, we can react quickly if the occasion needs it, to avert catastrophe: step gingerly away from a snake, smother a kitchen fire, flee from abusive relationships. Automatically absorbing a host of everyday details – putting on shoes, checking we have our purses and keys before we leave the house, turning out the lights – also conditions us to swallow trauma and get on, which can be helpful as a survival technique, to keep us moving.

If on the other hand, we choose to live consciously, most of the props of unconscious living are taken away from us, as we are invited to be fully aware of everything we are doing and why we are doing it, whether that is kicking playfully at a pile of leaves, working in a job we despise, living with a wonderful woman (or in a difficult relationship) or having a massage. Living consciously is at once extremely liberating, and extremely challenging, because we notice life slowing down to a snail's pace and every activity becomes, "What am I doing now, and why am I now doing it?"

If we were all living consciously all the time, we would move so much more slowly and carefully. It would become impossible to do even simple things without reflecting on them, so we probably would not do very much. The best compromise most of us can realistically manage is a blend of both unconscious activity, and conscious decision-making.

There's (unconscious) Joe, you see him? He is rushing to get to his car, so that he can drive away to work before eight o'clock and beat the morning traffic. With luck, he will be at his desk within forty minutes and can put in a good half hour before the phones start to ring…he feels nervous, excited, he anticipates, and hopes, and – God! – he wishes he'd remembered to finish his morning mug of tea.

Here is (conscious) Joe. He is sitting up in bed, stretching deeply, walking carefully to the shower, feeling the water on his back and on his head, choosing the soap, lathering and rinsing, wiping and cleaning the shower cubicle, padding back to the bedroom to get dressed, choosing his shirt, tie and jacket, deciding to have a fried egg for breakfast, savouring his morning tea for a change, kissing his daughter goodbye slowly and murmuring *see you as soon as I can, Princess,* before he leaves. Walking down the stairs and out the front door, he admires the new colour in the trees, breathes deeply of the fresh air, looks up at the sky, decides to take the bus, walks quickly…

Suddenly, everything is for us to choose. There are so many choices, so many tiny decisions to make and alternatives to notice, that it is little wonder we so often take refuge with the things we have always done and so often thought.

I have often used reactive techniques to survive difficult short-term changes, leaving bad situations in a hurry, for example, or huddling under the blankets, or pushing past a bad experience onto the next thing on my "to do" list without giving myself time to reflect on the choices I have been making. Reactive behaviour has its uses.

Eventually, though, we do need to take the lid off coping behaviours and process the situations we find ourselves in, if we are to learn anything meaningful from them. Unless we have the courage to do this, make the time and invest in some discipline for the reflection that this process demands, there is also the significant danger that we will never see past a network of blame that is at the heart of reactive behaviour and relationships. (While we react, we do not see ourselves as in any way part of the cause of a situation.)

Without intending to, I have found myself unconsciously putting the blame for situations on other people or on Life itself. *I ran away from her because she was a bully; I don't think this situation is working out because it's not giving me what I expected it to; I left that job because I could not stomach it; I have run out of options...*the list could continue into infinity.

I do not doubt that leaving, escaping, quitting, have often been the best I could manage at the time. As I say, reactive behaviour has its uses. But whereas reactive living tends to assume that *other people* are either responsible for what happened (to you) or that *other people* owe you something – an apology, an explanation, action on your behalf, courtesy, kindness, money, consideration, food or their energy – conscious, creative, deliberate living is clear that we are at the heart of our own lives, responsible, capable and able to choose for ourselves.

No-one owes me a living. No-one. Not my parents, not my spouse, not my kids, not my colleagues, not my friends or neighbours. If I expect something from them I am saying I can't stand on my own two feet. (Forgive me if you got this point a long time ago – it is one of my particular challenges, as I have always felt I don't actually stand on my own two feet, not confidently, anyway.)

Personal responsibility sounds good, doesn't it? Hey, I get to do whatever I like, when I like. But isn't it kind of scary too? If everything is up to me, I can't blame anyone else or lean on them, or expect from them…There may be things happen that I have to deal with. All by myself. Can I manage that? I don't know. But there is only one way to find out, and meantime, on the road to discovery, there is no reason to leap unprepared into the void, sell our earthly goods, emigrate or confront the boss while he is in a meeting…I can be powerful in small steps, in gradual increments. Awareness is the key that turns the lock, to open the door: awareness of our power, of our ability to choose, and of our core strength to direct our own lives. Most importantly, with personal responsibility and freedom comes the acknowledgement that the best way to solve a problem is not to create one in the first place.

In response to any set of facts or circumstances, then, my only decision is, what do I choose to do about it? The choices we make are not always immediately obvious, or easy, or straightforward, or fun or simplistic, but they become our choices, and our ownership of our choices unleashes a truly enormous power which we can use – as we choose! – to take ourselves deliberately to our next best outcomes.

HELLO FRIEND

I enjoy looking closely at the smallest thing. We can all do this and notice that our hands are amazingly agile or that our breath is a miracle – quietly in and out all day, never a fuss. We might glance up at sunlight streaming through that window over there and reflect that each pane of glass is a triumph of technology that keeps our homes brightly lit during the day. Out of the window perhaps the sky is a sweet, deep blue or there is a beautiful sunset drifting into depths of darkness. Maybe next door your child has finally gone to sleep and you just found her, her arms thrown above her head in a pose of perfect peace.

Looking at things in such a way, we appreciate even the smallest blessing in every second. This is bound to lift our "feel good" vibes. I have to admit, no matter what mood I am in, that electric light is a truly fabulous invention and I am incredibly lucky that I can access it with the flick of a switch. I turn on a bathtap and in minutes can be soaking in warm water. Do we know how much inventive technology has gone into these simple activities? Do any of us recollect how hard it was to achieve a hot bath or shower fifty years ago? A*ppreciation* is a quality which makes joy.

Appreciation leaps over fences and hugs our neighbours, too. Honest appreciation of the myriad wonders in daily life allows us to look a person straight in the eyes. When we go to an exceptional event, a concert by our favourite musician or the opening of a new exhibition and cannot help talking enthusiastically to the person next to us, we are crossing the barrier, emphasizing what we have in common. Reducing all our activities to a slower pace allows us to notice, to savour and take our time; and it is natural then to want to share our joyful discoveries with others. It is this easy to transform our understanding of life.

When we slow down, we also have time to notice how we are feeling and how others feel too. If we look carefully into strangers' eyes, over time it becomes harder to generalize, especially when criticizing groups of unknown others. Have you ever noticed, for example, that when we are in a bad mood with someone or determined to feel angry, we avoid eye contact? If we looked in the eyes of the person we are cross with or yelling at, we would see hurt, bewilderment and confusion. We avoid eye contact to keep our bad moods going. Self-hatred monologues too, *I hate my legs, my nose is too long, I wish* *my hair were different, I hate my life…*are very hard to maintain when we look in the mirror. In our eyes we would see all the hurt that these painful beliefs cause us. We would not speak so unkindly to our friends, would we? Yet many of us regurgitate words of self-hatred for years.

You may say that you "hate" someone. It is more likely that you hate the fact that they haven't understood you. It is my experience that "hatred" more often stems from fear of being misunderstood. There may be people who read us wrong or may even tell us they hate us. They may never understand us, no matter how hard we try to get on their wavelength. It feels horrible to be misunderstood and it doesn't help that when we would like to set the record straight our attempts to explain – "I was being perfectly civil, I wasn't frowning at you, I am sorry if you misunderstood me" – often make a tricky situation worse.

Should I bemoan my fate, rant and rave, lose my temper and make a vow of vengeance? A stubborn sense of injustice wants to balance the scales. You hate me, I hate you! It feels better…for a while. Just before my anger threatens to destroy a fragile peace, in the nick of time I reflect that if someone dislikes me I can select a consolation prize. It may be easier to agree that their feelings about me are…mostly their problem. Why should I make their problem mine? I do not have to share any decision to dislike and I choose for myself how I react in any situation. The more love we can offer in any situation, the more our love comes back to us.

To re-assess the whole idea of "them" and "us" at some point I stand a little straighter and realise, "I AM them!" Instead of forever blaming nameless others, I can choose not to play the victim. By staying resolutely calm and cheerful – by continuing to enjoy my life – I immediately become part of the solution rather than the problem. And friendships can come to me, because I am calm and in a state of mind that does not turn away from chance encounters, but blesses and appreciates serendipity. It doesn't always work, of course, but it is something I aim for and reminds me that every opportunity is precious. If all else fails, at least I might stay silent. Keeping a dignified silence, we resolve to be gentler, kinder, more understanding, though it can feel as if our heart is breaking quietly when we are misunderstood. It hurts. We all desire to be loved as we are.

Once we stop judging others it is so much easier to leave ourselves in peace and simply enjoy the gifts our lives have to offer. Feelings of humiliation when I fall, for example and tear my trousers or ruin a good pair of shoes, come from my own judgments about what other people are thinking. I imagine they must think I am a drunk, annoying or shameful in some way. But not one of these judgments, these thoughts

I believe others are thinking, is real; I am merely being prejudiced against myself. Maybe passers-by feel confusion or awkwardness that they cannot be more helpful. But none of that reflects badly on me. So now, if I fall, I simply get up again and focus on getting back to happier feelings as soon as possible.

Even though I know and have seen that self-abuse and self-hatred never make anything better, often I am unkind to myself. If, in a moment of optimism I were to buy a large piece of chocolate cake (you may say, "What is the problem?") and eat it all, I would suffer a sore stomach, a headache and sore joints, so eating cake is not a loving thing to do. But if I slip, sometimes I get cross with myself and feel angry or guilty instead of just accepting that I would rather not pay for the privilege of being ill. When we laugh at our failings, immediately we feel hopeful again.

Once we notice how often we pre-judge encounters, we see that many, if not most, of the divisions we set up in ourselves or between ourselves and other people, are erroneous. We unthinkingly erect a fence or a glass wall because we assume, perhaps from the way that someone glanced in our direction one time or because they forgot to send us an invitation to their party, that someone doesn't like us. You know, it is possible that they weren't looking at you, they had just lost their contact lens; or they were stressed out with being up half the night wondering what to do about their crying baby. If I'm honest, it is easy to recognise that most such doubts I harbour originate with my own insecurities, which, because of their private nature, I am prone to exaggerating.

Surrendering all thoughts of whom it is I like or don't like, with all the reasons that come attached, gives me a much easier time. Without enemies there is nothing to defend, because we begin from the happy assumption that no-one is attacking us. An alert, peaceful attitude means that, happily, we are less likely to be attacked. When my bitterest enemy notices that I no longer avoid her, she can't paint herself as my victim and has less to feel upset about. She actually starts to respect me more and leave me alone, because her desire to make me suffer has been deflated.

No matter what is happening out in the real world, I feel much freer when I begin with the assumption that all people are equal but different and that most of us just want to get through life being as happy and as peaceful with each other as we can. Even when I suspect this may not be true of particular individuals, because I begin with an assumption which is benign and inclusive, outright hostility rarely crops up. When it does and I am unable to resolve it, at the very least I take refuge in a dignified silence so that my antipathy does not blossom darkly around me. As a very practical tool for making living easier, my only question is: how do I choose to feel now?

None of us, no matter how wise or far sighted, can know what importance another person attaches to the things we say or do. We seldom receive positive feedback, especially from people we aren't intimately acquainted with. If we begin by treating others kindly even when we think we have nothing to gain, new opportunities arise for friendship, exploration and discovery.

LIVING IN BLACK AND WHITE

The habit we have of making comparisons stems naturally from living in a physical world, where we have to choose all the time. Choices and comparisons reflect the fact that we are all different and interesting to one another. When we invest our choices with flavours of good or bad, better or worse, it is an easy step to saying, "I wish I/you were not so…" and before we know it, we may find ourselves thinking in this way all the time.

Many comparisons we make, though by no means all, have close ties with normative language, the language of morality, which tends to be heavily basted with expectations of how we are supposed to behave and with sentiments which rely on words like "should", "could", "need to", "ought" or "must". Used continuously, words such as these end up taking the role of little bullying sticks, insidiously adding fuel to the fire of every encounter or conversation.

Judgments of different behaviours, habits and preferences almost inevitably follow, which often carry the implicit belief that we know how others "should" live their lives better than they do. If you don't think mere vocabulary could make any difference, experiment with using words like "can", "will" and "could" and feel the change in yourself. I have taken out a personal ban on "should" "ought to" and "must" and make a deliberate effort not to use these words or others like them. If some have slipped through my trawler net for this book, please get a big fat pen and score them out.

Making comparisons which carry judgments often damages our relationships, though the damage is often insidious and can be hard to notice. We become better off or worse off than someone (everyone!) else in our lives. Others' lives seem better or worse than ours, as do their kids, jobs, ideas. They are lucky, lazy or complacent…or they are poor, wretched, pitiable, lost, abandoned, unlucky… Judgments of this sort are not a good way to see anyone at their best. We may admire another because s/he dresses well and looks ridiculously healthy – better than us. We do not see them, we see their clothes, immediately either feeling envy or regret that we didn't think of that killer combination or smug because we went "one better". We resolve that next time we will "get it right".

With thoughts like these constantly harping on in the background, we are in a very unstable place. The ground is forever moving and we move up or down with it, up to the heavens or down in the dumps. The emotions thrown up by constant comparisons may feel sharp, real and invigorating, which offers us an excellent excuse to continue this kind of behaviour. Like habits born out of volatile relationships, one of our rewards comes from an adrenalin rush.

However, since we never know from one hour to the next how we will react to anything, the continuous emotional instability is hard on our bodies, our minds and our deeper sense of self.

If we get caught up in this addiction, we rarely appreciate the meaning of a smile or feel the warmth behind words or listen with calm attention. It may be a long time before we realise that our friends no longer confide in us. Maybe they don't care to invite us to their houses or don't much enjoy our company.

If you are familiar with this habit, don't worry. It is a small matter and can soon be put right. Why wait until tomorrow? We simply have to recall and remind ourselves when we are in situations that bring out this tendency: no-one is looking at us or thinking about us. Everyone is far too busy living their own lives to care what I might be thinking or doing, wearing or eating.

Sometimes it does matter what others think about us, for how else could we make meaningful connections or become aware of the need for change? How else could we get a job or convey an idea? However, for the present it is important to move away from the belief that people are really that bothered with *looking at us* or that any comparisons they make with us are bound to be unfavourable or even that unfavourable comparisons matter. Let's get our minds away from this type of thinking and into something more rewarding.

When we decide we no longer care as much and take the decision to climb off the see-saw, awareness dawns that defining our lives according to what we think others think about us is pointless. In any case, what we think they are thinking is rarely true. When we feel vulnerable, do any of us ever actually *check*? Would you ever go up to somebody and ask, "Excuse me, but are you thinking that my bottom looks too big in this dress?"

When I finally realised that many comparisons are meaningless and arbitrary, I gave myself a gift. I started to see myself as I really am and to love everything and everyone a little more sincerely. I learned to enjoy small pleasures: easy meals, walks in the park, a chat with hubby after a day's work. Food tastes better and even the fresh air now feels friendlier. I'm living in the real world, where even my simplest preferences are imbued with more honest joy.

Finally, I have started using comparisons the way

they are intended to be used: to wake and stir my senses, to allow me to be discerning in my choices and to enliven my day. When I use comparison to enjoy what I experience – have you ever eaten ice-cream and *hot* chocolate sauce? – I come closer to an awareness of the many pleasures in life waiting to be discovered. On our journeys of discovery, we all step gently away from the race against others and learn to walk in our own way. Eventually, we dance in the street for all we care and everyone can join in.

If being free to be happy with yourself just as you are is not enough of an incentive, your new freedom from "what (I think) others think" also illuminates what you *truly* most enjoy about life and where you believe your joy might take you. Giving yourself permission to *do what you like doing* and enjoy what makes you happy whatever anyone else may be doing, opens your life wide to new meaning and direction.

FINDING LIGHT

"The light is *in* you. Darkness can cover it, but cannot put it out." (10)

From infancy we are taught and are expected to come to terms with the complex laws of the physical world we are born into. These laws form our non-negotiable frame of reference. Thus night follows day, black and white are opposites and if I kick a football in the air, gravity pulls it back to earth, where it will land with an almost perverse exactitude in my neighbour's back garden. We also know that in our heavy, physical world, time passes at a precise, measurable rate. We often visualize our time as having a past, a present and a future and habitually view our choices as either predetermined or limited. Birth is painful, life seems to be a process of accumulating disappointments and death is final; all that sort of thing…

    I believe that when we start out life as babies we come into the world filled with lightness. We are naturally alight. Learning to live unquestioningly within moral and rational frameworks accepted by those around us, it is natural that we gradually adapt to the heavier physical realities which we see working everywhere. Indeed, so faithful is our acceptance of our world's physical laws that we often invest our spiritual world with the same beliefs we lean on in our daily lives. Thus, we humans tend to accept that the Gods of our belief surely see things the way we do. Naturally we hold ideas of right and wrong in our heads, so it is difficult for us to see our God behaving any differently.

I find it deeply puzzling that debates about spiritual truths are often heated and pursued with such vehemence. Labels like Christianity, Buddhism, Islam, Hinduism, Sikhism, Atheism and Agnosticism tell one part of our human stories; and although we need badges of belonging and identity, I believe that the things that define us should be as benign and as loving as we can make them. We all have to come to an accommodation with our lives, after all. If your spiritual identity gives you a gentle home, which allows you to seek goodness, happiness and a path to greater understanding and peace, it is working for you. If your beliefs condemn you to suffering and others to unhappiness, perhaps they could be re-examined. There are plenty of spiritual truths to explore.

Fate and predestination aside, all of us happily accept free will when it comes to our everyday, practical activities. If as countless philosophers have suggested, free will is an immutable law and gift from the Universe, is it only to be useful for the limited, passing practicalities of our existence? Is it not possible that *all* the seen and unseen aspects of our lives might be influenced by what we choose to believe? Seen in that light, arguments about faith suddenly feel rather futile.

If we have each come to our faith and understanding of the world through the exercise of our free will, which speaks to us from our individual experiences, is there any purpose in hotly disputing another person's spiritual standpoint? Is it possible that, in the same way that our expectations about our material lives become what we experience, our spiritual beliefs, all being fuelled by the same creative energy, themselves create countless million spiritual realities, all co-existing and constantly evolving?

What we experience as our earthly and spiritual reality is probably a miniscule part of the total realities out there. As far as I can deduce, the worlds of Earth and Elsewhere run in parallel; and the Bigger Picture holds many Earthly and spiritual truths spinning around us constantly, suspended in an ocean of light.

Spiritual laws do not come into conflict, but merely manifest themselves in our lives, depending on what we believe. The variables are infinite; and, of course, it is your free will to choose what you believe. My aim here is not to spark a controversy, but merely to suggest that spiritual laws are more complex and thrilling than we are usually aware. Many universal laws are constantly at work affecting the process of creativity. Ultimately, each of them can enable us to live lighter, freer, happier lives.

CAUSE AND EFFECT

There is a very basic law of the human world and of the wider cosmos, the rudiments of which we know and accept easily. When I do something, I cause something else to happen. When I speak to you, you answer me. When I go walking, I get exercise. If I am late for work, my boss is cross. If I cook a pudding, it is hot when I lift it out of the oven. Yes, yes, we know. If you are wondering where I'm going with this, please bear with me a moment longer.

If I am cross with my friends, they are cross with me. If I misunderstand you, you will fail to understand me. If I am impatient, life feels itchy and uncomfortable… At heart, we all understand the basic "give and get" mechanism here, even though many of us overlook the central part this process plays our lives. We like to think that we can be very crafty, clever or savvy, but that everyone else is an idiot. Or maybe, that it's all right for me to be grumpy and unyielding, but the rest of the world "knows" I am really a great woman. …Uh, no, sorry, I tried that. It doesn't work.

When the basic mechanics are pointed out, we quite easily accept that cause and effect are bound to have an impact on what we do today, tomorrow and next year. How else would we be able to plan anything? But consider how exciting our lives become if there is even the remotest possibility that cause and effect also move within all our belief systems. Most of us, in the everyday mix of what we get on and do, think it is downright spacey to suggest that these laws operate not only in all the places we see, but also in all those in-between Universes that we have never seen, in galaxies and places without number that we never glimpse, except perhaps in dreams. But why should we not cast our net a bit wider? What if we dreamed that, in every dimension imaginable, free will and cause and effect are working together inexorably to make our world? How would that change our understanding of our personal power?

MAGNETISM AND MATTER

Earth is a magnet with a very powerful magnetic field around it. Many of us may already know this. "And so what?" you might ask. If Earth is a magnet, everything it contains must also have its own magnetic field. Every person, animal, cloud, leaf, blade of grass, piece of wood, flower, bee, book, shoe, desk, table, stick and piece of fluff has its own magnetism.

A magnet attracts its own kind of "stuff". At a very high level, energy gathers together groups of similar particles which form into matter. Matter: those solid, edged objects we think of as being heavy, unyielding and dense. Yet, if we look through a very strong microscope at any object, we will see spaces between the molecules and micro-particles we call matter. If we look even deeper, we see that the molecules themselves are made up of energy or light. So, in higher reality they are not dense at all. They are filled with light.

From any desire that seeks greater personal awareness, we can apply principles of magnetism to explain why life unfolds as it does. We may be giving off good energy, happy vibes. By doing so, we attract similar energy from other people, places and even objects. Since we are magnets, we make the best of life by choosing cheerful friends, happy thoughts and interesting ideas and we might like to guard our negative thoughts carefully. When I feel negative, I attract similar negatives to me. They just come in on the same frequency that I am on. And as this is an attraction-based Universe, I attract what I am thinking about, whether I like it or not.

I asked my husband Eddie, "If there are two possibilities before you, one less favourable and one more favourable, which one would you focus on?" and he answered, "The less favourable one. Then I could do something about it," which surprised me. I would prefer to choose the more favourable one, since I know that by thinking about a thing, I make it more likely. The scenario we turn our thoughts towards is drawn towards us. Repeatedly, my experiences demonstrate that pessimism, sadness or anger only bring me more of the same. Although there may be times and circumstances when my optimism looks foolish, I prefer to hold out for a positive outcome whenever I can.

While we live and breathe, we cannot help applying our focus and our energy to something. By being indecisive or unclear about what we prefer, we constantly shift the goalposts. As a consequence, outcomes and possibilities are harder to predict. Whether we are happy to accept "what happens to us" or would prefer something different, constant shifts in our attention constantly alter the possible outcomes that show up for us. The secret of success, then, is to focus on what we desire, then keep our attention there: to stop changing our minds. When we act clearly, deliberately and without reservation the power of magnetism really gets to work for us and the results can be transformative.

MIND OVER MATTER MAKES OUR WORLD

Everything starts right here and now with what animates us: with our spirits, our thoughts and that part of us which has the clearest vision of what lovingly serves our higher purposes: our souls. Life energy – spiritual energy – is the origin of all things. From inspiration and beliefs come ideas and thought; from thoughts come words; from words come actions; from actions is matter made, brought to Earth and anchored here. From the matter we make, we constantly reshape our beliefs and so the cycle of creation continues. What we have in mind shapes our lives.

Again, we know more than we realise and in our language there are hidden many clues about creativity and matter. We say, "It doesn't matter," which means, we will not make it important to us. We will not make it (into) matter by giving that matter our attention, by drawing it to us, by importing it into our lives, by giving it substance.

We are unused to reflecting that our spirits are the origin of what we are, yet the shortest pause to consider must show that this is true. Whoever believes that the body, this mere casing of flesh, ever *governs* the spirit? The body is a mere *thing* which is animated by our spirit from within. Indeed, we all know that our spirits spark our bodies into life and that "death" is the absence of the spirit from the body. From a spiritual viewpoint, death is the dropping of the body by the spirit, but from either the spiritual or earthly viewpoint, Spirit is the spark at the start.

Just as the Earth spins peacefully on its axis and pulls matter into its orbit, our energies attract into our orbit circumstances, people and events which match our frequency. Mutual attraction works exactly like that. The hundred-and-one things in our lives – our partners, friends, employment, material circumstances, our emotional defaults and our assumptions around all of these, are with us because we are living at a similar frequency which brings them towards us and makes them matter to us.

What we each attract into our orbits varies widely, depending where our usual frequency is set. At the frequency at which we are humming, magnetism brings us what we "expect". If I am used to existing on a heavier, low frequency, I find that I attract lots of difficult circumstances and awkward people. A pessimist finds plenty of evidence to justify his attitude.

The same process is at work in the lives of realists and optimists and for every shade of person in between.

So if I want to get away from a "bad" situation that continually repeats itself – as they tend to – I must first realise that I have the power within me to change. Then, taking my courage in both hands I resolve to lift myself up. Hopefully, I start by releasing limiting beliefs and giving out more forgiving, relaxed and loving thoughts which will, given a little time, practice and patience, form lighter patterns around me, helping to shift my habitual frequency a little higher. Lighter patterns attract newer, lighter, brighter ideas, thoughts and outcomes; and so positive changes continue, each sign of progress feeding and reinforcing our hopes for progress. By loving myself more and envisaging better results, I am already attracting improvements into my life.

As an added bonus, those experiences that used to come in on the lower frequency naturally avoid me. As I am no longer on their wavelength, I no longer attract them into my life. For example, I may have been in an uncomfortable relationship with someone for years, depressed, overweight and lethargic. If I feel frustrated and unhappy, I have probably been living on a low frequency. Then one day I notice that the sun is shining and I reflect that I would like to smile, for a change. Deciding at last to take some control over my life, I start an exercise programme, go out every day and watch the weight finally fall off my hips as I gratefully resume my natural slimmer shape and size. I feel a bit better. I am more confident of my next steps and I revel in the long–forgotten feeling of being powerful and happy. Feeling new hope and cheerfulness, my frequency rises naturally.

Taken aback by the changes he sees in me, my partner says, "I don't recognise you anymore! You are not the woman I moved in with…" and the attraction that was there between us gradually peters out. If we are no longer attracted to friends or lovers, they drift away from us. In this way a natural process of renewal occurs and has the added advantage that in the process of changing we do not feel as if we are tearing ourselves apart. Our material and emotional circumstances evolve naturally to match what we feel comfortable with.

THE LAW OF REFLECTION

What we believe is what we see reflected back at us. What we believe then becomes the famous self-fulfilling prophecy, kept in place by the energies we emit. But the well-kept secret is that belief comes first and we can choose what we believe.

Imagine you are standing by a lake of crystal clear, calm water. In the water you see your face. How would you like to look: calm and happy, with a sparkling smile and a clear complexion? Or grumpy, sad, weeping and morose? The glass mirror of the lake cannot deceive. What you see becomes real for you.

If we want to see a beautiful reflection wherever we look, we do ourselves an enormous favour by cutting out cursing, swearing, blaming, complaining, martyrdom, self-pity, bullying, bossing, passivity, impatience, anger, boredom, regret, worry, fretting, obsessing, copycat living, envy, greed, intolerance, hoarding, acquisitiveness. The list goes on. All these behaviours have their origins in fearful thinking, which operates at low frequencies. Lower frequencies make life heavy and bring extra challenges we can probably do without.

While cutting down – and out! – anything that fills us with dread and clouds our horizons, we can all choose to use and dwell in those qualities we admire, such as cheerfulness, kindness, overlooking difficulties, letting go of tiredness, feeling optimistic and brave, giving and receiving thanks and praise, reserving judgment, feeling gratitude, generosity, patience, tolerance, peace and forgiveness.

We are free to choose what we like, of course. Experiment freely with any aspect or quality that you desire more of. Say, "I am free", "I am healthy" or "I feel ecstatic". Statements starting with "I AM" are wide open, allowing light to flood freely over any "problem" we face. The beauty of "I am" statements is that they are:

~ Very powerful: the first creative impulse is "I am": I am in control of my life; I am a strong and confident creator of my future; my thoughts, words and deeds are powerful...consider how these statements make you feel. If you feel suddenly liberated and happy, you are on the right track.

~ Wide open: they do not commit us to any particular course of action or set of circumstances.

~ Statements of our intention, declaring what qualities we see in ourselves, what hopes and challenges we accept and plan for ourselves, where we would like to go or what we desire to receive. Stating our intentions clearly brings our ideal future closer.

If our private or business circumstances are less than rosy, compare how we might feel saying, "I AM POWERFUL" with "I have a wonderful job". Saying, "I have a wonderful job" if I don't think I do, probably feels stupid and dishonest and might well put me off the whole idea of choosing to say anything at all. Guilt might get a look in too: perhaps I would feel that I *should* have a wonderful job and foolish or cross with myself that I don't. Such feelings are hardly helpful.

I find the "I AM" format clearer and easier to use, as it works closely with recognition and allows a more open formula to help us towards success without judging our actual circumstances.

You can begin a process of renewal any time. Now would be excellent. When you are just about to slip down the scale to bored or depressed, every time you feel like having a good old moan, repeat with feeling, "(*now I see that actually*) I am so lucky." In fact, try saying that whatever happens and feel luck and optimism bubbling up. Like a charm, when we say, "I feel lucky!" the dancing twinkle-toed chancer grinning inside us jumps up with glee. Say, "I am very blessed!" and smile for emphasis. See how you feel after a day, then a week and then a fortnight.

When "I am so lucky" – or blessed or peaceful or kind – becomes our usual response, we are indeed lucky, blessed, peaceful and kind. These qualities grow with each day that we allow them room to expand alongside us. But please don't let me tell you what to do, experiment. At the moment I enjoy saying, "I am incredibly lucky." Luck conjures up all kinds of adventure and excitement. What is round the next corner?

WHAT WE FOCUS ON GETS BIGGER

"To sympathize does not mean to join in suffering, for that is what you must *refuse* to understand." (11)

Getting to grips with this idea is one key that opens the door to a whole new way of living. What few of us realise is how deep this concept goes or how far it takes us. Where shall we start? Well, how about getting the heavy stuff out of the way first?

You hate your job? Stop thinking about how much you hate it! I admit, if someone were to say, "Stop thinking about an elephant dangling from a tree," I would think about an elephant dangling from a tree… Even so, knowing what I dislike allows me to deliberately move away from that. I can also purposefully resist the temptation to dig in and stir it up, since I notice that the more I think hatefully about something I hate, the bigger and fiercer my feelings get. I often experience this. From force of habit, I can feel myself doing it too, going down into old grooves and increasing bad feelings by continuing to insist upon them.

Any subject matter inevitably grows in size and importance according to how much emotion and energy we invest in it and the Universe does not recognise any distinction between "good" and "bad" energy. *Negative energy counts.* That is why we need urgently to cultivate a lighter attitude towards those things that upset us, as well as turning our valuable focus towards pleasant, even delightful, preoccupations. We are fearful for our jobs and we lose them. We worry about our health for twenty years – instead of having fun – and we end up diseased. We are so used to thinking negatively that I suspect we don't even notice when we are doing it.

Most, if not all, of our negative thinking and behaviour has one underlying cause: fear.

- fear of being condemned;
- fear of the unknown;
- fear of death;
- fear of pain or suffering;
- fear of loss;
- fear of being abandoned;
- fear of not understanding;

- fear of being misunderstood;
- fear of not coping;
- fear of failure;
- fear of lack;
- fear of not being good enough;
- fear of not being loved…

The list is truly infinite. When fear lies beneath what we think and do, the results are predictably poor. If we worry that we never have enough money – surprise! – we never do have enough money. Our most ardent, even our most modest and unassuming, hopes for prosperity cannot help us, if they come from and are wrapped in feelings of our lack, like a beggar's entreaties. With that attitude, lack and misfortune are what befall us: a great big zero. Worse, if we think our life is going downhill, it does that too. While we are cowering fearfully, expecting disasters, they crop up all over the place.

Our fears and insecurities are not the only obstacles we place in the way of our finding peace and serenity. If our hopes for personal fulfilment or financial success are visualized as happening sometime soon, perhaps for the next rainy day or when we retire, these hopes are for a better future. The chances are that our dreams cannot materialize. How could they? Tomorrow never comes. A similar thing happens when we wallow in the golden glow of yesteryear. Our present day seems dim and unrewarding by comparison.

Well-meaning and often afraid for the future, we may mournfully ponder all the dreadful stuff: the oil slicks, the fallen and destroyed trees, the starving refugees, the poor and oppressed. Burdened by feelings of overwhelming, intractable difficulty we create our excuse to do nothing. We say, "There is so much wrong with the World, what difference could I possibly make?" and walk past, fretting or wringing our hands. Even when we pray, the litany of the disasters we pray for sounds more like a never-ending list of the desperate and lonely rather than a prescription for sending serenity and love out to others. When we have the courage to bathe ourselves and our dreams in love, compassion and acceptance, we help make everything better. We always have the freedom to release fears that no longer fit.

Can it be that obvious? Well, yes, in a way, it is. The enormity of our task lies mainly in the sheer number of us who live our lives governed by fear, the number of times we let fear rule our decisions in an average day and the number of paralyzing dilemmas which would benefit from a more cheerful outlook.

When I see a world full of hurt which I know can be beautiful, I like to remember that every single positive thought, decision or action makes a difference as I take small steps towards the recovery of beauty, *in the right way.* It could be something as slight as picking up a piece of litter or adding a little more to my charitable giving every month. One small step at a time, we have the power to change the world.

Whatever obscenity I witness, whether it is a hungry mother begging or an abused child, it is a great deal easier to offer help when I adopt a stance which agrees, "I am loving and I share my love with you," than if I stumble past, avoiding eye contact and hoping that the beggar does not see me feeling overwhelmed. If the world is in a mess, how did it get like that?

Our power is perfectly able to focus on practical and *joyful* ways to make a difference; and to work with us to achieve that, at a pace that is comfortable and relaxing for us. When we know of a difficult situation, we can think of it lovingly, while visualizing and affirming the beauty of what can be. So, in our sympathy for the oppressed, we can invite visions of beauty and peace to surround our concern.

See wonderful things happening in your own life, in the lives of all your friends and also in the lives of all your enemies: the notion of "enemies" is based in fear. Fill your thoughts with activity, change and movement in a better direction; consciously start to feel relaxed, peaceful and purposeful. Dare to dream of peace and see the world mending. Stretch out good feelings all over the place until you see beauty overflowing, trees growing in great, proud forests, clear water and abundance. Have a vision for all these things based in love and you do make the world a better place. The more you envisage success, the more you see it, the more you find it. It is a great circle. It is a great circle and it can be even grander. If two people focus on a good outcome, the effects are more than doubled. If three people do so, the effect is more than trebled. Imagine the power that is unleashed when hundreds or thousands of people are all thinking good thoughts about a situation at the same time.

In the same way that we can notice and focus on the belief that we have plenty of time, we can notice we have plenty of everything else too: health, great choices, relaxing freedom, deep peace, loyal friends, artistic talents. *It depends where we are standing when we are looking out over the scene of our lives.* You can make a feast from two thin slices of bread and a small piece of cheese; you can have the holiday of a lifetime with just a rucksack on your back.

When "positive" becomes the default we choose, we learn that any situation, whether "good" or "bad", offers valuable insights. When we learn to see even our mistakes as helpful, we at last recognise that what we take from *any* situation is up to us. When I react "badly" to anything, I make it worse by piling on the guilt and self-abuse. Weaknesses are often illuminating, even amusing, and what I choose to take from a situation is up to me. I *always* have a choice.

WHAT WE RESIST, PERSISTS

This saying feels like an intriguing contradiction. Over the years I have caught myself wondering, what does it really mean? Sounds like a catchy idea, but how does it work?

Recently I was feeling sad: ancient memories of struggle were re-surfacing and I was losing the plot. Trying too hard had left my whole body aching and I was eating all the wrong foods and generally not taking care of myself very well. I felt like I was missing something that, by now, should have been obvious. It was time for me to face up to it…but what was "it"?

In the course of my life I have developed favourite "coping" strategies – who doesn't? At the top of my list is running away, which I have done repeatedly from many different predicaments. Standing alone in the middle of a busy high street, I was thinking I could keep alive the dream of running. Would it still work? Legging it clearly wasn't going to be possible for ever: I am not getting any younger and these days I have responsibilities.

Denial is also a favourite strategy of mine, but it takes a lot of effort to live in constant denial which is why, having let my guard down for a moment, I was standing speechless on the pavement while life swirled around me. I felt as if someone was saying, "Hey, this girl is finally getting it...she is just around the corner now...but my goodness, *isn't she slow!*" My patient friends were watching and waiting, while waves of comprehension seeped through my resistance and my tired beliefs.

There is a "third way". I can try to change my circumstances. This sounds really good, doesn't it? Change is what this whole book is about. Doing lots of lovely positive stuff has undoubtedly changed my life. Good prescription: strong on the positive thinking, empowerment, a worthy ethic for the modern era...But there are times, even now, when this way seems to demand so much effort and determination. Again, I felt as though I might have worked harder when I was younger and fitter, but on that day, choosing to actively embrace change sounded hollow: how do I change the fact that I have cerebral palsy? That I have always beaten myself up about being disabled, about not being good enough? *Change* by my own efforts felt too tiring and unrewarding to be the answer I needed then. Besides, I had worked hard all my life and struggled on, but frankly, the dividends were shrinking.

As another strategy, I have tried to change my perspective on being disabled, saying things like, "Well, it must have been intended, this, perhaps there is a reason for it...perhaps it does actually make me see things differently, make me more empathic, a nicer person..." Yes, again that is probably true. I have learned a great deal about empathy, withholding judgment, being gentler. Unfortunately, none of these consolations answers the heartache of being different, slower and unable to dance, though depending on my mood, they help sometimes.

This day, standing gazing up at the sky and oblivious of the passing multitudes, I realised I was facing something. Each of these solutions I had used but none seemed to work for long. So...there must be some other truth to discover that could finally bring me peace. As I got on the bus taking me home and was carried gently beneath the foliage of early spring, I asked the question: "What do I do now?" The reply was given quietly and gently. *I could try accepting.*

Eckhart Tolle (12) calls acceptance "surrender". For me, surrender feels more final, more complete than "acceptance", which suggests a polite debate over a cup of tea. Surrender is like the strong waves of finality washing over all the small, pathetic dams of denial I daily place in the way of WHAT IS. I finally understood that I did not have to struggle any more. I could surrender to What Is.

Now finally, I understand what it means when we say, "What we resist persists". Pushing and shoving – forcing ourselves forward while holding onto our difficulties – creates resistance. Resistance is struggle. Struggle takes energy. And since we are using and focusing our energy in resistance, we are making real what we are struggling against. Whatever we give our attention to, survives. Whatever we fight, we breathe life into. When we struggle for peace, our struggle fuels conflict.

On the other hand, when we surrender and totally accept any situation As It Is, the withdrawal of all our emotional "capital" makes the struggle evaporate. It is obvious that what we feed lives, and what we surrender leaves us. When we accept any "negative" situation which we are unable to change or work to our will, our surrender gives us what we have been seeking all along: peace. When I surrender to something I am not agreeing with it, nor am I endorsing any situation which is abusive or hurtful; I am simply accepting What Is. My conflict ceases, so conflict leaves me.

We are all familiar with the usual "coping" strategies: avoidance, denial, forcing change, persistence or altering our perspective. Each has its place. Each can make the difference between success and failure. But a coping strategy, no matter how brilliant, is only a short-term measure. My ultimate "problems" were not any I could change and therefore I faced the reality of surrender. In this I have finally found great strength, peace and certainty. Like the willow tree whose branches sway in the storm, if we have faced the inevitable and accepted it, we dance in the gale.

LEARNING TO RECEIVE

I increase my chances of finding happiness in many ways: with the giving and acceptance of praise; by saying thank you for all the wonderful gifts in my life and by seeing a good outcome. We each carry fresh strength within us to create an uplifting, positive reality. We cannot turn our personal power off, though many of us have forgotten we possess it; and often we ignore it, turn away from it or deploy it in ways that hurt.

No matter how far I may have progressed in my *understanding* of the principles of happiness using my reasoning brain, it is my painful experience that joy and success continue to pass me by unless I slow myself down, allow myself to notice good things unfolding around me, admit I would like to join the human party and consciously embrace delicious experiences and happiness for myself.

Perhaps the very first step in allowing ourselves to receive anything is *recognition*. Again, this sounds easy but progress is achingly slow, reflecting a past that excluded me from much happiness, personal pleasure and success. I recognise the many ways in which I have failed to allow success to come and stay with me. One of my older assumptions has been that *I am unworthy to receive*. Instead of confronting this painful belief directly, I have taken refuge with my old friend, appreciation.

I have been the world's most appreciative audience. Loving what others were having and doing may have set me apart from them at times, and often I have slipped into a vein of envy and hostility, but deep appreciation at least gave me a good place to start: I have laughed and felt good. I take great delight in looking at sunsets and being in thunderstorms. I love the beauty of nature and its powerful vibrancy. Where progress has proved more challenging is in understanding and accepting that all these wonderful things *are for me*, right here and now. Even this present second is bliss, if I recognise its blissfulness. What is the point of planning what I will do with my day *after* I have finished my bath? Instead of being impatient to get out of warm, luxurious water and "get on", why not simply accept that bathing is bliss? When I befriend bliss, it surrounds me in a warm, loving blanket.

When I see a lovely sunset, do I photograph it and e-mail it to a friend or do I stand and watch it until the sky has darkened, glorying in changes of colour and movement and thanking all the gods of the Universe that I was here to see it? Such beauty, as I watch it unfolding, makes me want to fall to my knees with gratitude. I am truly, deeply thankful for the refreshment that beauty offers.

Using my power to appreciate, a world in which I notice that I am free to embrace my own happiness has gradually revealed itself as the smiling, obvious choice, without any of the usual pain that comes when I force myself to confront feelings of lack of worth. Evidently, my attempts to persuade myself that I remain outside the circle of grace are entirely pointless. Sooner or later I am forced to agree that I belong within the magical miracle, just as we all do.

As an author who has had to do a great deal of promotion and networking, in my early days I was often preoccupied with the notion of success. Nurturing contacts, friendships and new ideas can be daunting, especially when we fear that our hard work may come to nothing; or worse, attract criticism. But I was working hard, and in that sense, every step forward was progress. And during that progress, I awoke to a powerful realization that unless I recognise now that I am now successful – in many different ways – I cannot be truly successful.

Like all the best ideas, this one is surprisingly simple. When I am forgetful, I overlook the obvious solution: it is my usual habit to scan the horizon for success, overcoming the hurdle in front of me without really noticing it and then saying, "Yes, but who cares about this hurdle? When I get *over that one over there, THEN* I will feel I have what I am looking for…I hope it comes soon!" Impatiently, I wait for my "success" to arrive. Why does it seem to float just out of reach?

I can stop that impatience in an instant, by paying close attention to feelings of accomplishment inside me right now. When I stay with any feeling which agrees, "Yes, I am very successful!" magically I see the elements of success all around me. Using new insight to appreciate my good fortune, I cannot help attracting more of the same. We can deploy the quality of gratitude consciously, to help reacquaint us with our good fortune. This process is not about feeling smug or complacent: Becoming more aware of any quality or aspect, our minds go automatically to look for it. This mechanism is simply part of how our world works.

The same is true of any other quality I would like to enjoy more of. If I wish to be prosperous, I recognise and appreciate that I am already prosperous and in doing so, attract more prosperity. If I wish to feel beautiful, I can hardly notice my beauty if I stand before a mirror bemoaning my ugliness. Yet that is what many of us do. We complain about our ugliness, our poverty, our failures while another part of us watches and waits, hoping to be recognised as beautiful, as richly rewarding, as successful.

I passed many years sleepwalking, unaware how much fresh power was waiting to be discovered within these ideas, within me. There is no need to wait. Scattered nearby lie flowers of beauty, abundance and good fortune. Our noticing them gives them strength, so that they grow and increase. Whether I like it or not, my powers of attraction cannot help pulling towards me what I AM. Thus, I deliberately choose to be – to feel – healthy, beautiful, lucky and fulfilled. When I recognise that I am all of these things, I cannot fail to be.

I realised that, "If I don't have enough to eat, I can get a smaller plate." Instead of gulping food down like a wolf in a hurry, I choose to eat each mouthful slowly, allowing space to appreciate the flavour in every morsel. By making a point of visualizing every situation as abundant and replete with possibility, we are learning to recognise blessings, a process that enables us to more easily embrace them for ourselves. It is the insight of a moment to know that abundance is a defining feature of life on earth. Everything which makes us tick is fundamentally about abundance. Life is abundant; therefore I have the inspiration, opportunities and energy to create a deeply fulfilling life. Life is abundant; therefore all my wonderful ideas bear fruit. Around me, the truth of statements like these becomes ever harder to ignore.

Once abundance is flowing towards me, the next step is to *accept it*. There is little point visualizing abundance otherwise. Unless I can see abundance flowing towards me and accept it as my own, prosperity turns away from me while others reap the benefits of my thoughts of plenty. In all likelihood, that type of lack will be a situation I have also created, as I unconsciously retreat to habits such as self-sabotage and forgetfulness. I can ask for it all: a loving and beautiful partner, a brilliant new job, more money and a wonderful place to live, but unless I happily accept these things for myself without guilt, they go to someone else. A*sk, appreciate and accept* for success.

Recently I hurt my back and found myself in the most unusual position of having to use two elbow crutches while walking ever so slowly around town. Walking with two crutches forced me to take things slowly. By the by, I noticed that for the first time in a long time, I had to ask for help with opening doors, carrying things and allowing extra space on the pavement to get past. Accepting graciously was a delightful discovery; and it occurred to me that I have lived a very self-sufficient life, constantly working to move on quickly because I was trying to do so much by myself. How often I have muttered, "I can manage, thank you" and continued alone and lonely, a method which has not been very fruitful.

If we hope to be any way successful, sooner or later we will find ourselves accepting help that others offer us. Asking for what we desire takes courage and practice. Accepting help from others with a gracious smile and a word of gratitude takes more practice, but is just as vital, if we are ever to be truly prosperous. Prosperity, like life, is a communal exercise. We all depend on help from each other. If we ask clearly, express appreciation and gracefully allow others to assist us, joy comes to us from every direction, any place. And none of this requires traditional effort of the kind we associate with success: no tears, no frantic action.

SELF-SABOTAGE

As I grow in confidence and the evidence of my success accumulates around me, self-sabotage is slowly becoming consigned to my past. I hope that very soon, it will finally release its hold on me, slip away out of sight and never bother me again. Yet, if I overlook it too completely, this destroyer of dreams lurks unseen and hard to spot, like a crocodile perfectly camouflaged in the riverbed. I need to know when it is nearby, so that I can step gingerly around it when I am fishing. Even so, the last thing it deserves is to be treated earnestly: bad behaviour thrives on being taken seriously. When we see negatives for what they are, we can decide to be gently dismissive of them. A little, light attention is enough.

Self-sabotage is that ancient conversation which quietly and endlessly repeats, "I can't *in all honesty* do this. What is the point, it has all been done before and *much* better than I could even attempt." It is the creaking voice of the aged cynic who has been telling me forever that nothing I do comes to any good and I will be dead soon anyway, so *why bother?* I would be as well to give up now, stop wasting time and just forget it. A master of disguise, this quiet, insidious bully hides behind "reason", "realism" and "common sense".

We all need to be a little practical when making plans, especially for the most inspired projects. The problem with self-sabotage is that, when it grips me, I cannot find any area where my projects or ideas are ever going to be good enough or worth persisting with. The self-destruct bug comes along and stops me from going the extra mile or challenging myself to take a chance – and risk failing – at something new.

In contrast to a happy creator who does what s/he does for the sheer excitement and joy of now, not caring so much about the results, self-sabotage has nothing invested in the joy of creative processes and is almost entirely preoccupied with likely outcomes. Therefore, this mind-set automatically finds fault with everything I would do that doesn't fall within clearly defined and well-worn parameters around what is acceptable, decent, safe, predictable, useful or necessary. It has the same messages to give me about *all* my new ideas, especially creative, splendid, whacky ones.

As I mentioned earlier, a while back I thought it would be fun to make up a compilation of songs. Perhaps I missed my vocation as a backing vocalist. In a burst of creative energy and optimism, I dreamed up new tunes and sang them all around the house, embarrassing the neighbours, probably. But I didn't care, because it felt good. For a while everything went well and ideas came to me in direct proportion to the amount of belief I invested in them. Then, just when I could see my creation on the cusp of being fantastic, like a perfectly ripe peach ready to fall into my outstretched hand, that idea came to a stuttering halt.

As youngsters we absorb the pattern of our experiences and then come to assume these are inevitable. We all grow up with what I call "Unhelpful Templates", lessons we absorb and falsely correlate, about the way life doesn't work for us. Equally, we can learn from Helpful Templates (loyalty is rewarded, love is unconditional, being together is fun). Unhelpful Templates include such things as believing that cruelty is inherent (perhaps we experienced cruelty), that absence is normal (perhaps we experienced a lot of absent parenting), that we don't deserve to be financially abundant ("Here's five pence I found on the carpet, that's my wages for the day...") and – two with which I am very familiar – that *Not Having* and *Having and Losing* are inevitable.

Not Having is the belief that I will never have what I want (physical freedom, physical ability, acceptance, friendship) because I have (falsely) concluded that being disabled excludes me from these things. *Having and Losing* even more painfully draws a false connection between achieving something and then losing it (the folk wisdom which says, "It will all end in tears"). I get a lovely toy (dress, holiday, time off…) and I am not allowed to keep it; I find a good job and six months later I am desperate to leave; I have a wonderful spouse and although I love him, we argue all the time and I am chronically anxious, though I don't understand why. Unconsciously assuming that Having and Losing were linked, I have until recently lived with chronic unease, falsely drawing the wrong conclusions from early losses.

Yes, I'm wistful and I grieve to notice all the false assumptions I have made. But such templates as these form when we are young, pre-verbal and unaware, so they are hard to bring to the surface and understand; and now that I am aware of Unhelpful Templates and understand about false correlations, I can breathe more easily and see past them to the power of choosing and building lots of new, positive and supportive beliefs, not choosing and losing.

Self-destructive behaviour can be part of a learned mind-set that is unable to accept any inherent value in new experiences, nor in what we learn when we experiment and risk failure. Historically, my fear of failure has run so deep that this bug would rather kick in my dreams before they become reality, than even take the risk of someone else crushing them. The farther I take a new, challenging project towards completion, the higher the stakes rise. Thus, self-sabotage works ever harder to protect me: hedging my bets against deeper disappointments; giving me all sorts of reasons why a thing is not going to work; turning up the volume when I choose not to listen; and as a last resort, making me fall and hurt myself, reminding me of my physical weaknesses or causing lots of stuff to go wrong. I drop things, they spoil. I crash around, forget stuff and lose important papers; all because my unconscious reaction is rushing to press the delete button before someone else does. If I sabotage myself, at least my failure remains a private loss.

My fearful reaction is working hard to help me, by reassuring me that if I would just be sensible, quiet, well behaved and *do nothing new* there will be no hurt and no sorrow and no-one need know about my pathetic efforts. Self-sabotage insists, "You needn't bother attempting this," and so ingrained is my familiarity with failure that, if I am not alert to the old pattern, I listen, nod my head and obediently slam the brakes on before *I get carried away and crash and burn in a mangled heap, the object of derision and contempt*. These particular cell memories are very strong.

A history of holding impossible expectations and

inexperience with feeling successful play their part in repeated failures. I have been given many gifts yet, with a streak of stubborn ingratitude, I have too often dismissed these as unimportant, yearning instead to tackle projects that were doomed to fail: walking "normally", trekking in the Amazon, climbing a mountain. My early experience was that I would try and repeatedly fail at impossible ambitions. A tangible inability to do the physical things I most wanted to do, as well as my insistence that only achieving these things would make me truly happy, created a deep well of frustration.

Doubtless, we all recognise this gremlin a little differently. As my friends comment wryly, I am very contrary, a trait which perhaps arose because I had so much to prove. I had to prove I could attend a mainstream school, that I had the ability to attend university and qualify as a lawyer. I have had to prove that I could work in mainstream employment, get married and have a child and that I could indeed be modestly successful at these endeavours. Even when I write books, there are some who say it is madness to waste my time, so I still have lots to prove. My contrariness has its uses, because when people say, "Oh, but you can't possibly manage that!" I instantly think, "Oh no? – Just watch me!"

But I notice that my combative reaction is unthinking and automatic. So, when someone says, "You can do this, if you like," too often I have just turned it the other way and thought, "Oh no, I couldn't possibly!" Too often I have launched straight into denial, rather than thinking through each suggestion as it comes along. Without understanding what I was doing, I have sabotaged even happy possibilities.

The articulate among us can dredge up endless well-argued reasons why a thing is *not* going to work. We may be unwilling to accept any possibility of easy or straightforward success, constantly censoring our hopes and feelings and adding disapproval into the mix. If something is "too easy" we automatically become suspicious. And making it public that we believe success can be ours, will, we fear, invite ridicule and contempt. Many of us also learn to accept and live with defeatist behaviour. There may be a lingering feeling that it would be shameful to do something badly or admit when we cannot manage something. I grew up hearing, "If you can't do a thing well, don't do it at all," and my school house motto was "Only the best is good enough". I was never going to be best at anything. Any time I got close, a cynical voice at my ear jeered and I gave up.

Unless we are alert and watchful for destructive patterns and unless we can devise strategies to deal with our fear, the end result is usually the same: we walk away from yet another project which once gave such a bright sparkle to our lives.

I also learned a rather unfortunate coping mechanism to handle my pain: doing nothing. The problem with this solution – have you spotted it yet? – is that doing nothing goes no-where. If fear of failure, of criticism and being judged is enough to stop us in our tracks, we miss out on learning some really liberating truths such as: the world is a lovely place; I can stay centred in bliss regardless of what other people think; and usually, my harshest critic is me. Most people will not criticise us if we do what we enjoy, they will probably not even notice. Some will be happy for us, a few may be jealous, annoyed or disgruntled. The vast majority will simply be enjoying their own lives.

How sad to miss out on the excitement of creating a lovely life, only because we are frightened to be unpopular, controversial or a "failure". In any case, doing nothing fails as a survival mechanism, because it provokes judgment and criticism – "don't be such a lazy bag of bones" – which are the very things that we are anxious to avoid.

All of which helps to answer the question why I allowed myself to simply *exist* for many years, but does nothing to shield me from the pain of noticing how many years I have wasted, how many chances for enjoyment and pleasure I have let slip, because I was frightened of criticism and because I believed that even if I was lucky enough to find happiness, I would lose it in the end. I have been treading water for decades, instead of relaxing and having fun.

We call this kind of behaviour perfectionism, defeatism, fatalism or resignation…it has many names. But it is learned behaviour, so we can unlearn it. When negativity rears its head and patiently and rationally explains to me, as if it is my wisest advisor, why what I am doing is not going to be "good enough" or worth the effort, I soothe that voice and then deliberately look for a way to step past it. A choice I make as a forty-five year old woman has very little bearing on fears that froze me into stillness when I was a child.

Now, when I choose to do something new – which my subconscious self understands is risky – I direct my thoughts towards seeing a successful result. I use affirmations, humour, energy, intention and sheer determination to just get on and make a start. I know that self-belief powerfully shapes every outcome; and staying optimistic feels better. I also release my emotional investment in the outcome and focus on simply being happy now.

Because I listen more carefully, nowadays I also notice that when I am fearful, my body aches. If, after deciding to do something new, my body feels like a pin-cushion, I ask, "What am I afraid of?" With gentle reassurance that there is nothing to fear, that loving support is around me and that the Universe is benign, usually I uncover the fear holding me back.

With more understanding and gentleness, the pain subsides. I still drop things, fall and break pieces of furniture. The trick is to look past all that and keep going. Hag to the rescue!

Whenever you hear discouragement or hostility in your ear; when something or someone is bullying you out of your happy feeling into a dead end of logic, *recognise bullying for what it is and gently but firmly ask it to leave you in peace.* Each time a bully stick rises up, threatening to beat the life out of you, recognise it as decrepit branch of a tree that has long been dead.

Doing nothing is not a convincing choice for a happy, fulfilling future. It is the small, half-baked solution of despair. As we all can, I am beginning to do fun things: taking risks with my writing, with what I say to people and with what I choose to do. I take chances, all the while supporting my hopes by recalling the joy and excitement that first inspired me.

It is the doing of what we enjoy each day that is most valuable, not whether we sell it. Doing what we love, having a go, makes us happy and even contributes to curing defeatism and illness. If, like me, you tend to fear the big picture with its dark horizons and unknown futures, focus on delightful details. If you find yourself tangled up in troublesome details, take a step back and lift your eyes to the longer view. In the same way that watching waves pounding the shore reminds us of the wider world, a broader vision keeps life in perspective.

We all worry. Some of us are so accustomed to the chatter in our heads that we have forgotten what the silence of acceptance feels like. If, having contemplated happily what I desire to do, I am clear that I wish to go on ahead *because I enjoy it and I am worth the effort* – yes, I am – the voices of doubt fade out, eventually leaving peace in their place.

We always have the freedom to release fears that no longer fit. Dismiss self-criticism and bullying with love and they finally make their peace with you. Gently reassure yourself that discouraging voices are insecurity or fear from the old times, nothing to worry about, now that you are growing and creating your own life.

SURRENDERING OUR ATTACHMENT TO RESULTS

Conversations with God (13) reminds us that when we surrender our attachment to results – the ways in which our choices turn up – our happiness is assured. Yet any suggestion that we need not concern ourselves with outcomes seems to flirt with an apparent contradiction: here we are, looking for and choosing good outcomes, expecting happiness. How can we be happy if we are unconcerned with results?

We do not change unless we see something we wish to change. We exercise differing degrees of practical control over our lives, yet we are always making choices and can choose to think, feel and act differently. In that sense, we are not disengaging from the outcome – not at all.

While inviting us to surrender our attachment to results, we aim to be clear about what we desire. For example, we can constantly adjust our life pictures so that we can feel and see ourselves being increasingly confident, carefree and happy. Once our stated goals are clear, fresh peace and certainty carry us forward. We can help ourselves further along by continuing to release anxiety, worries, problems or reservations about our choices. First we are clear, then we ask, then we stay with our intention. With that clarity, what we intend has a much easier time showing up, often in unexpected ways.

What next? If you are anything like me, ingrained habits of thinking and fretting will kick in shortly afterwards and very soon we are arguing ourselves out of our hunches, away from our newfound certainty.

The likelihood of success in any endeavour increases when, having thoughtfully made our decision and fixed our intention, we resist the urge to calibrate all the possible outcomes, attempt to grasp every different way forward or ask the fatal question, "Yes, BUT HOW can this possibly work?" The "ifs" and "buts" we send along with our desires cause unnecessary difficulties. It is indeed difficult to see how our clear intention to do something is made any easier when we then throw rocks of doubt onto the path in front of us.

When we have invested a lot of thought, effort and time in a project, naturally we care about the outcome. We want to succeed, but often our hopes are wrapped around with fears such as, "Gee, I hope they approve, I hope she likes it, I hope that this is not just a waste of time, I hope no-one criticises me." Fears of not being good enough and of disapproval stop us from committing completely to the joy of what we are actually doing now. I could sit here and think, "Oh, this book will never be perfect and I might as well give up, because there are so many books out there that explain this much better." That kind of fear, which feels very real, can easily stop me in my tracks.

To keep my fears and uncertainty in their proper perspective, I can set them aside for a while, go back a step and reconnect with the clarity and intensity of my original desire. Clarity and certainty create a strong current, pulling me towards fulfilment, thus helping to achieve the outcome I desire.

Happiness is found in what we are doing now, not in fear of what other people may think about what we have done. Taking action – without any concern about whether our hopes are practical or feasible; and regardless of "whether I will succeed", "what people will think of me" – is what matters most, in making real progress.

I find this fear particularly acute, but ultimately I welcome knowing about it. Learning how I may set it aside has taught me a great deal about the virtues of courage and persistence. I notice that this particular fear is both unreal and unfair. I am frightened about what people will say or do, when I choose to do something. I fear their disapproval. But they may be relieved I am doing something – at last! They may be happy for me, and filled with joy that I am making my own choices. Indeed, that is what I am discovering, so now I know that this particular fear is mostly a figment of my overactive imagination.

I wrote my first book because I felt impelled to do so. That book is published and I used to spend a lot of my time scanning online sites and social networks checking ratings, reviews and comments. Each day, as I powered up the PC, my stomach was in knots worrying about what others might think – *YAY! They love it, I'm happy! Aaaaw, they hate it, I'm sad....* And that felt very uncomfortable. The discomfort was telling me something, so I took myself firmly in hand and looked at this situation again.

Do I write in order to gain approval? Do I deserve only to glean my sense of self-worth from the variable opinions of others? Feedback has been overwhelmingly positive and encouraging, but there are those whose reading preferences have nothing in common with mine and whose motives I do not understand. Simply put, there is no need for me to invest my faith or sense of worth in any of that, because personal integrity and progress come from doing what makes me happy now, not from what might happen with it afterwards.

This is what is meant by surrendering our attachment to results. We go ahead because we feel good about what we are doing and we don't allow opinions or worries over practical priorities to send us scuttling backwards into the old refuges of fearful thinking. Whatever happens, whether we scoop the prize or have to start again, acting without fear of the consequences is one way to help the consequences come out right. When, assuming we are clear about what we choose, we relax, let go and learn to float, good outcomes arrive more quickly and easily.

To forget that we have made a request is better than remembering we do not have our answer yet. When we are going with the flow and doing what we enjoy – when we get on with our lives meantime – natural "default optimism" comes into play. Since it is hard for us to wait for our prayers to be answered without becoming disheartened, Life secures a happier outcome if we make a heartfelt request and then forget all about it. Here, forgetfulness is the way; while meantime, we do something – anything – to refresh and uplift us.

I was sitting by the telephone and I sent up a prayer that I would really love to hear from a friend of mine. I then forgot about my request and about thirty minutes later, while I was happily having lunch, the phone rang and it was her husband calling to let me know she would be contacting me.

I needed a new pair of elbow crutches. The

crutch I was using was old, the stopper slippery and dangerous. Rather than helping me stay steady on my feet, it was sliding out from under me. I knew that in order to obtain a new walking aid from the hospital I would need to set up an appointment with my GP, visit her, get a referral to the local hospital out of town, go to that appointment and argue my case for some assistance, all of which could take weeks. I could also purchase a pair online. In any case, I sent off my request to the Universe for some new crutches and promptly forgot all about it. The very next day I "just happened" to be standing at the kitchen window when I saw my new downstairs neighbours throwing out two brand new elbow crutches that had been abandoned by a previous tenant. My husband rescued these for me.

We were on holiday having an early supper at a highland resort when the rain started to come down hard, hammering the pavement. We had not thought to bring our coats from our car which we had parked some distance away. I was wondering what we would do, so I asked for help, then forgot about it and got on with my meal. After we had finished and were leaving, it was still raining heavily. We saw a covered golf buggy drawing up alongside the entrance steps. The driver kindly offered us a lift back to our car. That ride was such fun.

I noticed I had only one cheque left and then I

promptly forgot about it. The next day as I was working at my desk, I saw my chequebook and thought, "I must do something about that," so I telephoned the bank, where the chap who answered said, "We sent a new book out to you yesterday."

I can be clear about my hopes for the longer term: "Please can I move to a lovely new home, with a conservatory and a room where I might write in peace?" and, since that is a clear, heartfelt request, the Universe immediately goes on the lookout to help me achieve that. If, having made my request I later come over all apologetic or argumentative, saying, "I shouldn't be silly, I only have a small pension"; or if I then attempt to control the process by insisting that our lovely house has to have a built-in sauna and a double garage off the main road or that everything has to be sorted out by next week, the situation becomes needlessly complicated.

Insisting on telling the Universe where the answer must come from, I limit the options needlessly. In any case, universal laws are not capable of being manipulated and do not succumb to threats or emotional blackmail. Far better if I decide what I choose and then let the Powers that Be sort out the rest for me. If I am not concerned to predict the ways in which my choices show up, I accept that answers may arrive unexpectedly from anywhere. Surrendering my need to be certain of the outcome of any endeavour and allowing myself to move forward regardless of what other people may think, I open up endless creative possibilities and unusual solutions I could never have dreamt of. If I trust outcomes to sort themselves out, they come to me from everywhere.

WHAT IS NAÏVE ABOUT OPTIMISM?

Ladies and Gentlemen, boys and girls, I bring you long-awaited news which shall be for all people: LIFE IS TO BE ENJOYED NOW.

Just for some gentle amusement, let us make a contrast of three different types. They will all be familiar to us. We know, however, that they are merely caricatures.

Mrs. Pessimistic was brought up to be very careful. Life has been hard for her because it has been hard for her, because it has…She doesn't publicly laugh at people's jokes, in case that would be unseemly. She is resigned to wearing the same clothes that she was wearing fifteen or twenty years ago since, because life is hard for her, all her money is spent before it comes in. She worries at night that the planet is in a bad way. Her neighbour has warned her repeatedly about the nasty boys who live in the estate nearby and there has been a spate of bad break-ins recently.

Mrs. P has not had a holiday in ten years, except for the family's modest excursion to the coast last year. They spent eight hours in the car in a horrific traffic tailback. It rained constantly and there was little enough to be cheerful about, God knows! They argued all the time – their son is troublesome. Mrs. P suffers from mild depression; she has constant low backache and sore knees and last week she fell and had to go to the hospital for x-rays. It cost a lot in taxis and the doctors said there might be some traces of osteoporosis. She feels like crying every day. There is nothing to look forward to in life.

Okay, stop, I think that is probably enough. You get the picture and I could go on and on. It is rather depressing to write this: it almost begins to feel real again. There is so much sludgy grey around here, no wonder poor Mrs. P feels unhappy.

Mrs. Realistic likes to see things just as they are. She prides herself on her realistic approach to Life, which is Unpredictable. It is best to Be Prepared. Mrs. R has a good laugh now and then with her friends, but nothing that would be over-the-top. After all, there is a lot that needs fixing in this world and it would be unfair to get carried away by a sense of happiness when many people have so little and there is a great deal of suffering in the world.

Mrs. R managed two vacations last year, one to the family home in Southampton. It is in the old part of town near the sea, which is nice, but not everyone has that privilege and she is grateful. Mrs. R has a part-time job earning just enough to make it worth her while going out. Her daughter is in college and hopes to get her diploma in legal studies soon, so that she can get a good job and settle down with her man. She is realistic about her prospects, too. She has her feet firmly on the ground. A nice steady job…

I think that is enough, too. It has about as much flavour as a wet weekend in a phone box. You can be so realistic that you feel half dead before you have started living! It doesn't feel very colourful, does it?

Mr. Optimistic is a real pain in the leg (according to Mrs. P and Mrs. R). When will he grow up! He goes around wishing everyone a wonderful day. It was sleeting last night, for goodness' sake! He laughs constantly and appears less than concerned when others are miserable. He is forever saying he has a great life, doing the thing he loves most in the whole world, which is looking after his infant son Josh.

His wife loves her work helping to run a local art gallery, which she does most days. Josh and Mr. O go out to the park together and slide down the big slide right to the bottom. They eat sweeties on the way home, while ambling and looking at the birds, the grass and the lovely puddles and mud. They talk about everything and hatch plans to have fun each day, because life is better that way and time passes easily. Mr. O sleeps well at night and enjoys intimate relations with his wife, with whom he has been in love now for over fifteen years. He has cordial relationships with his neighbours, who think Josh is a wonderful child. They offer help all the time. Mr. O has no problem paying the bills and if finances are tight this month, he knows that they will be better soon. Mr. O sees life as a big adventure and often the magic of life takes his breath away.

Okay, who found Mr. O too good to be true? Most of us? And yet we can all choose how we react when faced with "reality". Surely it is better to be as positive as possible and add colour to our lives in this way? There are many who would like to challenge me on this and quite rightly. So, let's take a really bleak scenario and see what we can make of it.

Maybe I have been dumped down a dingy hole by a bunch of kids who want me dead and there is no immediate prospect of rescue. Well, maybe I take the opportunity, for certainly I have the time, to sit quietly and ask for help. Then I could try to calm my fear by thinking good thoughts, perhaps focussing on how wonderful I will feel when I am free. I may try to visualize myself in a good place and plan what I will do to improve my life when I get out – I might as well. If I am able to calm my fears and see things positively, I am inviting creative solutions to my side, which increases the chances of getting out of my hole. I might be able to see a way of digging some steps into the wall of the pit I am in. Someone may hear my cries for help. Moment to moment, my life is still a miracle.

Am I really suggesting a hole would be a good place to be? No, of course not, but surely in any situation it is better to flood myself with "feel good" feelings rather than "feel bad" ones?

I have never yet found myself in a hole so deep that there is nothing I can do to help myself climb out of it. I may feel that life is more pinched and difficult, more troublesome than I would like. In that case, why not reinvent myself as an optimist? If our circumstances are flat or unrewarding, or we feel trapped and at the mercy of other people's demands, maintaining a relaxed, peaceful attitude may be the only positive contribution we can make to our situation. In the midst of anger, boredom and pain, instead of meekly shuffling along in grey, I can still choose to be all the colours of the rainbow. Humming my favourite tunes doesn't cost a thing. Instead of seeing my jar as half empty or nearly dry, I can see it brimming over with joy and laughter, with the golden nectar of possibility, my possibilities that I create with my desire, with my intentions and with my built-in power.

If you don't believe that your life is a miracle, go and find a map of the solar system in an atlas or library. Look at our galaxy and ponder the sun. Ponder the miracle that placed our Earth at exactly the right distance from the sun and, uniquely of all the other planets swirling around in the Milky Way, gave us exactly the right alchemy to be living here, now. How does that feel?

If that doesn't work for you, reach back through the years and recall the thrill of looking up at a blue sky when you were six years old. There was nothing "unworthy" in your feelings of happiness then. Happiness is not worth less now, just because your age is in double figures.

PESSIMISM HAS ITS PLACE

Okay, well, I don't believe that. I just wrote it because it works…you know, optimism, pessimism, the whole swing from there to here and back…That shift and change is part of life, a very normal and necessary part. And if you play the game right – not the way I played it for decades – you can successfully use your negative emotions to guide your actions, just as you can use your own happiness as a barometer for your success.

Without negative emotions it would be very difficult for us to decide what we prefer. Dislike is as much a guide for us as fondness and joy. I dislike being miserable. Therefore I choose to be happy. Simple… Ideally, we would like to arrive at a place where we make confident choices and see their results flowering everywhere. But since most of us will not reach that saintly plateau where serenity and peace are our constant companions, since we all experience negativity, we might as well make it our ally. If we are going to give anger, resentment or depression house room, they are going to work for their keep.

Anger

Anger comes from being frustrated and fearful of making changes. We want to change, we want to move and do something different, but are afraid; and instead of admitting that even to ourselves, we get angry with the world, with our children, with our partner. Within anger there is a core of truth that we are forgetting. Being unhappy and not knowing why, we hurl our unhappiness outwards at other people.

Am I angry with you because you have not done what you said you would? Or am I angry because I am tired, or because I believe that other people are sabotaging my hopes by their selfishness? Is my partner rude to my parents? Are the neighbours thoughtless?

Our negative emotions reveal where we are failing to flex our own emotional power. I feel anger when I am not doing what I would prefer to do, not saying what needs to be said, or suppressing feelings that are desperate to be released. Typically, this means I will have invested others with the power to influence my life and make choices that I should be making for myself: I wait for answers and approval from my friends, from my parents. I wait to hear from colleagues and peers instead of getting on with my life. Feeling powerless then makes me angry and I blame "them", instead of standing firmly on my own two feet and doing something to help me deal with feelings of frustration, whether that means going for a swim, choosing to go for a long walk, taking the day off or making that phone call.

To stop blaming other people, to stop waiting for them to provide my answers, reminds me to retrieve my power. When I love and approve of myself, my power reasserts itself naturally and my anger evaporates. When I bravely go ahead and choose to do something, I may make mistakes, but so what? Indeed, it is only by making mistakes that we learn anything. That is rarely fatal. I am always learning, beginning again; and when I feel myself going in a direction I would rather not, I can alter course.

Likewise, what other people may think of me or what I am doing is not necessarily so important and certainly should not be my excuse to stop, again, or derail my cherished ambitions. Other people may be critical and their opinions may show me in an unflattering light. Even so, these usually have very little to do with me personally and say more about their own motivations and issues, about which I probably know very little.

At the end of the day there is nothing I can do

about anyone else. They have their lives to lead and their own choices to make. But me? I am a powerful force to be reckoned with in my own life. I can decide for myself. Not all the time and not always alone. But yes, when it matters, I can decide.

Living in a world which is a mix of opposites, the challenge is to plot a course through all the available opportunities, using our intention to be clear about what we desire. We may pray or ask for clarity. Sometimes, the challenge is to reach out to others and risk asking them for help; but whatever we are doing, we have no option but to choose. We navigate our way continuously. Now and then we simply have to find the courage to stand and walk forward on our own two feet.

Depression

Being depressed is often a sign that our anger is turning inward and eating into our body. It latches on and clings around our neck, over our shoulders, pulling us down. Stepping away from depression feels difficult. The good news is that, more often than not, we know what is making us depressed. Since depression is a sign of long-term unhappiness coming home to roost, we usually know too well why we are sliding around in the darkness. Our sciatica is getting us down; we would appreciate more help; we don't think we will ever find a lover; we can't seem to settle in a job that we enjoy. Or we really want to find a home where we can be free of abuse, of controlling parents or noisy neighbours. We know all about our problems, but can't see a way out of the dark tunnel.

The way forward into the light is to listen to what our heart is trying to tell us and have the courage to act according the truths it reveals. Rhona is a friend of mine. She is very bright, an innovative thinker. Her mind is a treasure of originality and joy. She skipped maths at school because her mother thought that would be best. Even so, she went and got a degree and then worked in a shop where it became clear that she was bored and wasting her talents. I said, "Go back to college and study," and she listed ten great reasons why that would never work: she had a student loan; she had to find the money to pay the rent on her flat; she also needed money to live and she hadn't the time both to work and study. All my suggestions were thrown on the altar of common sense and burned. So I left it.

I caught up with her later on and she tells me she is studying engineering, having done an access course to gain the qualifications she needed to pursue her first choice of studies. She is near the top of her class. She is happier and more fulfilled than I have seen her in years and she can't stop smiling. And her student loan, her rental payments? Her problems may still be there, but they no longer block her way to a life that she is choosing for herself. Rhona has decided that her happiness matters to her, and it does: being happy whittles our problems down to their proper size. When we are happy, our problems no longer dominate our horizon. Our good feelings show us solutions we could not see before, because our blocks were keeping them away. Rhona's student loan may be paid off in instalments, the noisy neighbours may move away. She may find the lover of her dreams was living across the road all along.

Worrying

Does worrying make anything easier to deal with? I doubt it. Because the energy we emit has magnetic qualities, worrying draws what we are worried about closer to us, making problems more likely to materialize. Our worry also acts like a ring of static noise, keeping away solutions that might suggest themselves. We worry, perhaps because we believe we are alone in the Universe or, that God – whatever that might be – has better things to do than bother about us.

Imagine that each of your worries is an empty glass bottle, and you have quite a handful of these. Notice the heavy containers that you have no use for, that are filled with nothing but air. They are empty and bothersome, they take up a lot of space and they make a lot of noise, clanking around. Worrying about empty bottles obviously has no effect on them. When I was a kid, I could return these bottles to the shop and get some money back on each one. So, how would it be if we could hand in our worries at the counter which is always open? Just like a normal business transaction, without any guilt, sorrow or worrying, we tell the storekeeper, "I am going to hand every last one of these worries over to you," and for each empty bottle, we would get a full one back, just like that. The bottle we accept in return is full of the solution we seek...

These days, when I have a worry, I hand it over and get on with what I am doing. I know that I will get my answers, in good time and in the best way to take the next step. It is comforting to know that I am surrounded by help which delights to come to me, simply for the asking.

Sorrow

Genuine sorrow is nothing to worry about. We may be feeling immensely happy and fulfilled and then something comes along that cuts like a knife and makes us deeply sad. This happened to me recently, and so suddenly. It felt weird to be so happy one moment and then so deeply cut into by a sorrow the next. But sorrow is good. It frees us to feel genuine grief and pain, it releases us to express our love for others, and we should never hide it or try to pretend we feel less sorrow than we do. Honouring how we feel is such an important part of expressing our truth; and expressing our emotions openly – and calmly – is part of what makes us unique and special.

Resentment

Negative emotions that live within us for many years become second nature. Some, like sorrow, weeping, yielding, worrying, manipulating or apathy have a soft quality. Others are harder, like anger, hatred, aggression or resentment. Resentment was the dressing-up cloak that I wore, which allowed me to pretend that I was happy being excluded from games, that I wasn't very fond of physical activity and was delighted to be left clutching a book most of the time; when actually, being active in the open air is one of my greatest pleasures. The deal I made with my warring parts many years ago was, "I don't want to drown in misery, not yet, so I am going to put the fence up. I am going to be hard." At least, being hard, I didn't sink away to nothing. Resentment made me sharp-tongued, unkind and objectionable, though almost anything was better than constant grief.

It was relatively recently that I asked, clearly praying for help to be released from the bumpy upset

I was feeling. I could not articulate what was causing it, but I longed to escape my self-imposed isolation, to re-join my family and enjoy a peaceful, gentle life with them. I knew how I felt and what I would prefer, so I made a sincere request for assistance and got on with living.

Very soon, I was shown how I had first learned to use resentment as a survival mechanism – it was better to start out hard because then, at least I could keep going. Resentment helped me to move, but I hadn't realised that it became a huge part of how I saw the world. I got so used to carrying it around that I forgot it was in front of me like an enormous, distorting mirror. It grew so big and heavy that all my working systems reflected off it, slightly warped, but nevertheless, accepted by me blindly as "the way the World is". Like other coping strategies – denial, anger, acquiescence – resentment is best used for a while and then released. Instead, it became a permanent fixture and an uncomfortable fit. I found tiny offences and small objections in the most commonplace interactions.

Unconsciously resenting everything, I saw how I was creating my own difficulties in seeing every innocent act as deliberate, targeted and offensive. It was the seeing of the offence that was wrong, since the offence was not there. Throwing out resentment in reply, I was creating my difficult world. Being shown such a clear mechanism to explain where the resentment originated in my life has allowed me to drop it, lower my defences and soften. At last, others can relax and be themselves with me.

Guilt

Given the maze of tortuous feelings I navigated through earlier life, I think it is fair to admit that a seam of complex guilt has been a big part of my puzzle. Perhaps, in being born disabled, I drew one conclusion very early, that I must have done something terrible in a previous existence. To be acutely aware of what I would prefer and consistently unable to reach it… there must have been a reason for the quiet torture. Without understanding why, I punished myself with constant self-denial and with my obstinate refusal to embrace love, peace, satisfaction or joy.

While exploring the effects of guilt and seeing how widely it overshadowed every aspect of my present day, I felt in danger of drowning, not only because personal cruelties I inflicted on myself and others were being revealed after decades of concealment, but also because I understood that, in all that time, I might have been so much happier. I am not naturally resentful or depressive. To combat rising disbelief and sadness, I repeated quietly to myself, "You are allowed to breathe deeply, you are allowed to sleep deeply, you are allowed to eat enough, you are allowed to laugh out loud..." but in the stillness, the recognition of all the petty sufferings I put myself through was hard to take.

My search for answers has taken me to healers. First, to counsellors and therapists who provided a listening ear and allowed me to understand much within a safe, accepting environment. Then to doctors and from there to alternative, more holistic practitioners: nutritionists, chiropractors and osteopaths. More recently, I consulted a spiritual teacher. What he advised, I already suspected, though I was unable to express what was holding me back. My heart leapt with relief as he explained that I have a good, strong energy centre, which starts out with a great, bright burst of enthusiasm. But, after its first strength and optimism, it stutters and gradually fades away, repeatedly. How true this felt. This is what guilt can do, because guilt and resentment have a deeply PARALYSING effect. If there is one thing you take away from reading this book, please understand that acute guilt stifles life and stops us from reaching achievements that would refresh and delight us.

As part of the process of clearing away the guilt, I searched for something to lift me clear – there was no way I was I going to expend any more effort *going through* everything! Whatever worked would have to be something about getting away from guilt, clearly, but the only word I could think of was "guiltless" which, since it contains the letters g, u, i, l and t, would obviously be less than effective. It took some days to recall that the opposite of guilt is innocence. If I am not guilty, I am innocent.

When I say "I am innocent" with firmness of purpose, when I repeat this and assure myself of my right to feel at peace, the fog of paralysis begins to clear and feelings of failure, frustration and loss slowly evaporate. The punishments and the pain which go along with guilt and anger are slowly becoming a thing of the past. Finally, I can have fun. Finally, I am happy.

PROGRESS AND PAIN

I know that I am making progress. Some months ago I woke up and was going about the usual household chores quite peacefully. As a matter of interest I asked, "So, why am I sore all over?" and received an answer: *anger is being released.* I remembered that yes, come to think of it, I had indeed asked to let go of anger and Spirit was delighted to help with this process.

As I had watched my daughter playing one afternoon, I glimpsed another world in which people are not angry all the time. How I longed to be like them, not carrying this sharp weight around with me. So, right there, I had said a prayer out loud, heartfelt and certain, voicing my clear desire to be gentle and to release my family from my anger. I looked again and saw with clearer eyes, the way things are for them. They just want to have a good time and be happy; *and so do I.* I said sorry for all the hurt and decided to drop anger as any kind of excuse to push happiness aside and trap myself behind my own fences.

Life is fleeting and time is a precious gift. Soon my daughter will be grown. How do I want her to remember me? My husband may become very busy. Will I lose the chance to be happy with him? Opportunities to be happy with them are valuable and every day is a fresh chance. I recognised their desire for happiness and knew that I wanted to rein in my own angry habit. That was my decision.

And then...maybe you have read this before...I started to get ill. I got a stuffy head cold and a cough. My left foot ached and the ankle swelled up. I had to raise it up to take away the heat and puffiness. I looked up Louise Hay's book (14) which is still a favourite. *Left side = receiving side, receptiveness, willingness to accept, to welcome, to embrace. Ankle = pleasure... Willingness to embrace pleasure...*that explanation worked well enough for me.

Why was I hurting? Possibly because I made the clear decision to release anger as a habitual response, my body ached for a few days as the anger that was located in me rose to the surface and was released. All the happy feelings that I encourage are still going into my cells to replace the old rubbish, but if the bowl is filling up with all the lovely new stuff, where is all the old muck to go? Out into the open, all over me. The pain in this process was the answer to my prayers: I sincerely asked to be released from anger, so it came into the shallows and gradually floated away.

Spiritual progress usually causes some kind of physical backlash. Physical reactions are sometimes my body's attempts to return me to a level of discomfort with which my subconscious is more familiar. When I'm trying something new and out of nowhere I develop aches, pains or a cold, I can help to subdue these by gently repeating, "I am healthy, I am healed, I am whole, the spring is eternal and my roots are deep" or "I dwell in bliss." Another formula I use is:

-Pain is just resistance to the inevitable truth of my wholeness;

-Resistance is based on fear and worry (but fear and worry are not real…);

-Only love is real.

By using gentle reassurance that the primacy of the spirit within the body does not threaten my body but only enhances its function, I recover my health and optimism more quickly than if I merely shell out for some painkillers and grimace. Gradually optimism reasserts itself.

Resistance is what the old mind-set offers automatically. The old mind is unhappy with change and only wants to return to what is familiar. But when our changed mind is clear about what it prefers, our new desires wage a gentle charm offensive which, little by little, renews the internal landscape and alters our internal points of reference. The new, happier mind is winning as all our understandings about what works best for us are gradually transformed.

The body releases negative emotions slowly, playing its part in this game of tennis that is change, resistance, recovery, improvement and on-going change. As you know, the longer we have held negative emotions the slower they are to be coaxed away. Eventually, they do leave. I may be sore today but I welcome that kind of pain which signals the release of lifelong patterns of immobility, frustration and anger. No wonder it hurts. Releasing pain frees up space in my cells for new - and welcome – colourful, happy memories of joy, peace and fulfilment that will never leave me and which console and delight me as I grow older.

TO HAVE AND TO HOLD?

It is a great pity we organize our lives with many rigid rules, as if we think we must hack out a way forward through concrete. The methods we have devised often appear un-necessarily inflexible and punitive, while all around us the currents of life pulse peacefully, ever changing and renewing. All of life moves in a constant state of flux.

Regimentation is largely un-natural, since it pre-supposes that life, which moves, can be caught in a jar or fixed in a state of permanence to a wall somewhere. Our sense of being in control remains largely an illusion, although mostly we are not aware of the illusion that we are working to make real. We are equally unaware of the strenuous effort that goes into keeping up a sense of order, though in the loss of our joy and the suppression of our spontaneous selves, our health pays for the pains we take. Only we humans attempt to superimpose this kind of "order" over life, a task which becomes heavier as our years pass.

I had a dream in which I was in a swimming pool. All around me the water swirled, while I would insist on trying to stand firmly on the bottom. Of course, such a stance goes against the nature of flowing water which was bubbling with ideas, my rigidity only creating problems as well as pain and difficulty for me. I was invited to remember that, for success, I should not insist on standing rigid or upright, but instead should relax. My body would rise through the water and float easily on the surface, all fighting surrendered. Then all would be successful – and so it has proved.

We are invited to notice that when we accept what comes to us, we are allowing abundance. Our striving through life, our "hard endeavours" create difficulties and barriers that we then have to work to surmount. With our struggling attitudes, it is as if we are building a wall and straining to climb over it at the same time.

The natural condition of our beautiful, blue planet is bountiful generosity and endless abundance. But somewhere along the road to our modern state it appears we have forgotten that this is how nature is. All too often we are taught to think that there must be a "catch" somewhere, that it is better to strive against nature, to conquer and subdue all our wilder impulses and the unknown, as though they are unnecessary, primitive or frightening.

Generosity lies at the heart and soul of the natural state. If you don't believe me, go to the nearest park during spring and gaze around you at the pink and white cherry blossom; stand beneath the apple trees. Each branch snaking peacefully from each trunk has hundreds of thousands of flowers on it, carrying millions of petals in unconscious splendour. Each park lawn has untold trillions of blades of grass. Wander to a beach and contemplate the rocks or the sand. Have you counted the grains of sand in a small handful?

In the natural world, teeming with untold millions of Earth's creatures, there is no such thing as waste. We are probably the only species having any concept of "waste", whether that is something surplus to requirements – and therefore somehow useless – or a substance which is toxic or hard to get rid of. Most other species live well within their environments, where waste is recycled naturally into more of what is needed. There is no distinction between what is useful and what must be thrown away.

We, in all our grown-up calculation, rather tend to view surplus as "wasteful" and to believe that if I have lots of something, someone else must therefore have less. Since we believe this, we run our lives accordingly and adjust all our beliefs to fit, hoarding what we have instead of sharing it. Thus, our beliefs in scarcity tend to become fulfilled. Because we have learned not to share, we have forgotten that sharing is ultimately in our interests.

In one part of the Democratic Republic of Congo there used to be an abundance of fish in the rivers, so there was rarely a shortage of food for local people. The rivers were also full of hippopotamus. Everyone just accepted that as the way it was and gave the hippo respect by keeping their distance. In recent years the hippos have been heavily hunted by men from outside the area using semi-automatic machine guns, with the result that now the hippo population is decimated and fish stocks have almost collapsed. Water quality in the rivers is also very poor, where before it was good. Why? Well, scientists have "discovered" that the fish thrived because they ate hippo droppings: the hippos had a waste disposal service, the fish were fed, the water was cleaned and the villagers were effortlessly catered for, with clean water and an ample supply of food nearby. There was no waste, no worry, not even a lot of work. Left alone, the ecosystem just revolved effortlessly, supporting all who lived within it. Disrupted, a self-renewing system that had been taken for granted quietly collapsed. We are just beginning to understand how fragile natural systems are and how complex is the balance that allows them to sustain life.

As a species we are becoming increasingly addicted to counting, measuring, assessing, quantifying and utilizing everything that we find, cataloguing it or sticking lots of dead specimens in museums, in drawers or in boxes. This habit appears to be getting worse and I suspect that it does us and the world we live in no good at all. I believe it stems, in part, from a worshipful attitude to money, which we also count obsessively as if it might get away from us were we to leave it to its own devices.

Scientists, conservationists, television executives, businesses, politicians, economists, teachers and pupils: we all seem to be getting in on the act. We count, weigh and measure everything that crosses our path: money, time, energy, opportunity, possessions. When confronted with the natural world we piously collect up species on the brink of extinction, then tag them and bag them. If they get away from us, we track them across mountains, rivers and forests with our radar devices, our cameras and our hot-air balloons. Television companies from Britain, America, France, Germany, Spain, Italy, India and China are all on the lookout for a rare and fascinating glimpse of the aye-aye or the snow leopard. In the name of knowledge, interest or entertainment, we look for rarity everywhere.

We do all these things with such good intentions, perhaps in the belief that our interest bolsters conservation efforts and provides harmless entertainment. We are *trying to help!* The argument goes that we need to know, in order to do something to reverse this or that dreadful decline or avert yet another catastrophe. Naturally, we all help by becoming more aware of the impact our activities have upon the planet and by assisting with restorative attitudes and action. We can also learn to listen more carefully to the quiet wisdom of the natural systems that support us.

And yet it becomes increasingly apparent that we do not really understand anything fully and see only a very small part of any puzzle set before us. What we do know, we think we understand. Then we go on to apply "solutions" which inevitably cause more problems than we could ever have foreseen. We may throw up our hands and say, "We meant well" and spend the next decades attempting to re-discover that gentle equilibrium which we tore into with such gleeful ignorance. Truly, in case such as these, ignorance is bliss.

The scarcity principle, according to which most of us seem to run all aspects of our lives, complicates this trend, since it revolves around the fundamental belief that there is a shortage of anything. If we could somehow seal up this belief so that it couldn't contaminate all our thoughts, its effects might be less harmful. Unfortunately, its logic is extended to everything: food, friends, free time, love, fresh air and all the soft furry animals on the planet.

Belief in scarcity comes from insecurity or fear. Fear prompts belief in scarcity and scarcity is fearful. It is another example of circular thinking, except that this one is a shrinking circle, unlike the chicken and the egg.

In writing about abundance I am met by a seeming contradiction: if there is lots of everything, how come there are shortages? And is it not complacent at best and damaging at worst to believe in abundance? I mean, look at the state the world is in. How can there be enough? Patently there isn't.

One part of my reply urges us to change our perspectives, to naturally value what we already have and appreciate all the wonderful gifts we receive. We are such a contrary species that it seems the more we have, the less we appreciate it and the less we have, the more we value it. In suburban Scotland, where food is delivered to our doorsteps from every continent, I feel as if I need a dozen ingredients to make a meal. On a remote island where there is one shop, I find myself grateful for half a loaf of bread, a scraping of butter, some jam, two eggs and an apple, with which I make a most delicious pudding to fill three people's stomachs.

And what lies at the root of a new appreciation? Our awareness that the Earth is naturally abundant. We can catch glimpses of this truth and when we do, our fears tend to vanish. Whenever we remove our fear of lack and loss from the equation, we gradually understand that there is no need for us to hoard our "stuff". We notice that small, daily amounts of what we consume are enough to live well. Indeed we would live well, being freed from the obsessive compulsion to acquire money and goods, none of which bring us lasting satisfaction. If I am hoping to be abundant and fulfilled, it is helpful to learn to appreciate what I have. When I wrap myself in feelings of appreciation, fear tends to dissipate like mist over clear water on a bright morning.

WE ARE ALL CONNECTED

When I write that we are all connected, I am not only suggesting that we all deserve respect. I also mean that fundamentally, what we do to others is, in the final analysis, *the same* as what we do to ourselves. We are all part of the *same big picture*, linked by and to *the same* spark of life and light that gives birth to plants, frogs, creeping insects and vast colonies of termites. And beautiful, fragile butterflies, busy bees, sinuous antelope, shy gazelle, secretive fish. We each look different, we behave differently from each other and we all have unique features. But our uniqueness is balanced by an underlying reality that everything living is much more like everything else living than we are usually aware.

I believe that when I hurt you, I hurt myself; and when I injure myself, I injure you. It is all part of a picture of reality which looks and behaves much more like a wheel than a straight line. Seeing ourselves walking along a straight line through our lives, we often reassure ourselves that we leave our less laudable behaviour behind us; in fact, the consequences of our poor behaviour have an un-nerving habit of rearing up in front of us when we least expect them to. Since we are all connected, it makes no sense for me to be deliberately rude or cruel, since I eventually feel the effects and suffer for my own thoughts. It has been my experience that deliberate cruelty I mete out to others becomes habitual and at some level I probably expect to receive pain in return, perhaps in remorse or guilt. Even if I do not feel regret, I may be living with a level of brutality that eventually reverberates around me.

A television programme I watched many years ago made a lasting impression. It took a rare and intimate look at the violence inherent in gangster culture in the townships of South Africa at a specific time. A former gang leader, who looked about seventy but was probably in his late thirties or early forties, was interviewed about a profound change that came to his life. In his youth, he had believed that violence was the way to survive the brutality he saw around him every day. He himself had suffered greatly, having spent many hard, brutal years in jail. Most of his friends were dead. Having escaped that dangerous time with his life, he finally realised that living violently was making everything else harder. He was sickened with his past life and decided he wanted to change. Now, as an old man, he spent his time telling young people that violence was not the answer, hoping to heal some of the pain he saw around him and desiring to make amends.

FORGIVENESS

Forgiveness may feel like a wide-ranging subject, so daunting that we can't get round to tackling it – so many mistakes, so much to forgive…It may feel easier not to bother. However, conscious forgiveness is highly effective for releasing much suffering and lightening our lives.

Although there are inevitably some people we are unable to forgive, when we can accept, even theoretically, that we are all fundamentally the same, it follows more easily that we are each worthwhile, acceptable and lovable. From the heart of such awareness, the beginning of forgiveness is possible, for everything "they" did to us and for what we did to "them". Forgiving ourselves may be especially difficult, but since "they" really does include "us", there is no real obstacle to forgiving ourselves and many excellent reasons to start now.

We do need to be aware that there are things to forgive, otherwise nothing can change. If I smack my children because I think they are naughty, I may sincerely believe that is what I must do to teach them how to be good. I may genuinely believe that if I spare the rod, I spoil the child. Or I may expend time and energy justifying my behaviour because it is too painful for me to admit that I have hurt other people who didn't deserve it. Even so, the longer I wait before making a move to change, the more accumulated pain I will have to acknowledge and the tougher it becomes to admit my mistakes as I work ever harder to justify myself. Continual reasoning of this sort takes up head space, absorbing a great deal of our strength.

We can make a simple start by *listening* to what others are telling us; not just with their words, but in all the ways they behave when they are in our company. Do they come to us spontaneously or do they skirt around the edges? Does my daughter feel able to say sorry for something she may have done? Something as small as how she laughs in my company is revealing. Do we give others time to talk in their own way? Or do we finish off sentences for them? Do we think we know what is going to be said, before it has been? Are we always planning the next clever thing to reply? Any of these habits makes it hard to listen.

We are aiming not to pre-judge situations. Judgment says we have already made up our minds, which is one reason why we stay in the same old ruts: if I have already decided something, then I am hardly likely to notice any need for change. If instead we hold back and wait quietly while someone is talking, gradually we bypass our old assumptions and internal dialogue about what someone *really means* when they are speaking. Letting go of our assumptions lets new light flood in, illuminating meaning that we may never have noticed before. If we are prepared to watch and listen quietly, perhaps especially to those whose opinions we would normally consider un-informed – for example, our children or our neighbours – whole new worlds shyly reveal themselves.

In undertaking finally to see and hear things *as they are* as if for the first time, inevitably, we may have to come to terms with changes in our understanding. We may feel unexpectedly emotional or even overwhelmed by what we discover. Seeking professional support in this process is worthwhile, as long as this does not reinforce any belief we may harbour that our efforts are endless and incapable of solution, a reverential attitude which makes difficulties much harder to release. Letting guilt and sorrow go, and allowing total acceptance and forgiveness to flood into our lives, is perhaps the single most important thing we can do to bring ourselves peace and happiness. If you are a practical person needing to be convinced, I offer a few reasons why forgiveness is valuable.

In many cases, our perception or memory of "what

happened" may be totally mistaken. If I was six years old when I saw or heard something which continues to haunt me, it is very probable there are external truths I cannot know. Why, someone may ask, did my daddy beat me? He said he loved me, after all. It turns out that this is what his daddy did to him, so he could not learn any other way to relate to children and is probably still frightened of the responsibility of looking after them. If – and this I guarantee – we cannot know all the reasons why something happened, it is best to let such memories go. To hold on to bad memories is to have judged someone and it is hard to judge well without the facts.

What is more, since we aren't able to go back and check "what really happened", why torment ourselves with something which has all the reality of a dark, cloudy nightmare? Of course, we may still feel pain and sadness. But sometimes these are old feelings we have chosen to keep alive with our memories, dragging them each day into the present and carrying them with us everywhere.

Let's imagine I telephone my sister to apologise for something I did when I was eight years old. Either she will say, "That's okay, I know you are sorry and I forgive you; I forgave you ages ago, actually." Or she may say, "What on Earth are you talking about? I don't remember that." If she says, "Yeah, that was a horrid thing you did, you spoilt my life!" I finally get a wonderful chance to apologise. Say sorry now, if you feel you need to, even if "they" don't want to accept your apology. Having then done your best, let the memories go. In being sincere and in taking positive steps to mend matters, you have done all you can for the present.

If we continually recall into the present events and assumptions that others have forgotten, our present-day reality and all our reactions *in the present* are filtered through those memories of the past. That is unjust to other people, since our behaviour is coloured by events they won't remember. In that case it is a fair bet that they have absolutely no idea what our problem is.

If everything we think, say and do is influenced by something which is no longer real but which we are recalling each day, our recall puts a distorting filter on any clean reality we might discover. Wearing old, dark glasses, we don't see the world as it really is, bursting with colour and potential.

Each day is new and fresh and deserves to be given full credit as an exciting opportunity. If we forgive someone we release them. Releasing others makes us feel very light, so release is good for us, too. Go on, be selfish and forgive someone today!

Having looked afresh at your life, you may honestly feel that, in fact, no-one has ever truly loved or understood you. If that is so, don't despair. There are countless opportunities to make new friends and as you let go of lots of toxic junk, you will find all of life becoming easier and more fun. There is one more thing you can do: make yourself your own best friend. When we care for and truly cherish ourselves, not egotistically but with an appreciation that we deserve to rediscover joy and share in the delights of life, we bring fresh light and energy to every situation.

You are free, as ever, to leave aside any thoughts that the re-discovery of your gentle, loving self is time-consuming, ridiculous or laughable. Decide to start over again. It is easier that you think. We can do meditations and visualizations to search for our young selves and bring them into focus. If this idea appeals to you, you could start by drifting back in your mind's eye, to an age when you were happy and smiling a lot. How old were you? What did you look like? In your mind, retrace your steps to that time and find a happy place, remembering what you felt like at that time.

See an image of your younger self, imagining details such as the clothes you would be wearing, your hair style and your shoes; invite your little child over for a chat. Give them a hug or sit beside them so that s/he talks to you in their own way. When I do this exercise I first reassure my young self with lots of love, saying that I want to be with her on her own terms and that I will *listen carefully to her* without judging whatever she wants to share with me. We might go for walks together to beautiful places. I visualize us, the adult and the happy child together and I listen gently, even when she tells me something I might not want to hear. We laugh and sing. We may make a date to meet again soon.

There was some pressure on me to be sensible and grown up young and I was pulled along by it. The little me who was earlier abandoned and left by herself as I grew older, now lives more happily inside my grown up parts, being allowed her expression. This makes (the whole) me very happy.

Even though I might have felt a bit foolish at first, by making this kind of exploration real I am bringing back playfulness into my days. There is more fun and frivolity "just because!" Playfulness and other child-like qualities, as well as forgiveness and understanding, surface more easily and more often.

In one of my most powerful visualizations, I found myself in a very strange, quiet place. Knowing that I have issues with frustration, aggression and anger, I asked for help. I had recently been made aware through listening, meditation and reading, that our subconscious stores every act of unkindness we ever experience. Although it felt daunting – there is a lot of unkindness in my past – this undoubtedly felt true for me; and I longed to understand the "how" and the "why" so that I could *stop* being unkind. Without understanding how I came to this, I felt like a thin spirit, being supported somehow inside a tree trunk! Perhaps because I love trees and have often made personal parallels with their rootedness, this image and device was suited to my lesson. On this occasion, the tree seemed to represent on the one hand, the physical strength and support I was going to need, for what I knew would be a difficult lesson; and on the other hand, the immobility I grew up with which might lie at the roots of my personal frustration and anger. I suppose I was being invited to lean into the tree, so that I could deal with the pain of what I was going to discover. But yearning to see this, I went willingly.

I was invited to go back and relive my life from age zero up to any age I felt I could manage. At any time I could stop the process. I went way back to when I was about nine months old. I do not consciously recall being that age, but I was able to feel how I would have felt and react as I might have reacted. All my nerves felt very near the surface, as they are for all babies, no doubt.

A little baby feels everything. Most things happened *to* me. Each act of unkindness is a thin layer of pain that drapes over the shoulders, gossamer light at first. Even at age one, the most innocent baby act is misinterpreted by others, which is easily done, since a baby can't say what it wants. At first the pain of being misunderstood is intense. Imperceptibly we get used to it and we learn to see past it. It does not go away, but lies over us, so that our gentle thoughts are obscured and our happy impulses become increasingly muted. The change happens so slowly over time that we almost do not realise. Even so, especially when we are small, we see what is happening and we are aware that this process of layering, with its particular kind of pain, is avoidable. This is why such pain is acute for little children, who long to be understood and be loved for who they are.

The process of assimilating pain unfolded slowly but relentlessly. Reaching a point that might be described as "age ten" I had to stop the process. I could not continue: I finally understood that pain accumulates. It does not go away. Each act of inflicted pain is retained by the body which receives it, causing grief. Pain and grief provoke a desire either to numb the senses or to retaliate. I finally understood why I was ever aggressive or hurtful and why I would want to stop resorting to such behaviour. I am more careful now, because I have been given the gift of knowing what it felt like to be a little child. And I do not want any child to carry a heavy mantle of grief. Especially when I can do something about that.

After all that honesty and hopefully having reached some better understanding and acceptance of who we are, we can gradually – or all at once – let go of the bad stuff: release it, send it out of our heads, out of the window, away with the birds or swept up by the sea. I invite you to take a walk by the shore and have an imaginary shouting match if you need it. Or write down everything you need to say and burn it or shred it. Let it all go.

In recognizing the physical and emotional relief and freedom that comes from releasing all the old stuff, all those heavy, stifling vibrations which clog up the body, I feel about twenty kilos lighter; I have much more energy since I no longer distort my strength like a dam that I have built and which I struggle continuously to mend or strengthen against the natural tides of passing time. Just think! I can throw away every mental catalogue of whom I am not speaking to and why. Some lists go back a long time. With more room in my head and my heart for what is happening around me now, I become much more receptive to the beauty of the present. Beauty, I notice, fills me with feelings of good fortune, joy and peace.

If you would like some practical proof, try this exercise. Think back to something in your past which still makes you cross or sad or which has left a hard lump of heaviness inside you. Perhaps there was a bad experience at work which haunts you or you feel anger from a long time back that you wish wasn't there. If so, start by gradually bringing yourself into a place where you no longer desire to feel *anything* about this: you dislike being repeatedly caught by negativity still held in that memory and you would rather not be affected any longer. If your aim is to think about new, wonderful things, just for a moment, try to feel that sense of freedom. Even if this cannot feel true for you now, dreaming of release feels good.

Next, before you go to bed, draw a picture of the problem on a large piece of paper. It doesn't matter what the result looks like, only what it *feels* like. Add any details or scrawls, scribbles or colours, anything you wish to make the picture feel as complete as possible. Colour it, cut it, mix it and add to it until your work is finished. Is it a mess of churning, black confusion? That's fine.

This process of contributing activity to intention puts your problem "out there", where it begins to evaporate. Draw a firm line around this problem's outer limits on the page, then stand back and say, "Is that all it is?" Say aloud, "It is finished," repeating the words until they feel true for you. If it helps to have a more physical image to help with release, visualize your aggravation as a large yoke of wood, which you finally sling off your shoulders with a grateful shrug. We are looking for a shove to start a process of release in your mind. Even if it takes a few days, set up a scene in which you see yourself washing away a stain, casting off rocks into the sea. Use any picture you like, one that feels convincing for you. Repeat,

"I desire to release all my feelings of anger and loss about this situation. These feelings no longer fit me. I release, I let go, I it is gone, I am finally free."

When getting off to sleep, over several nights if necessary, say, "This is ended, this is finished, I am clear of this and I choose to let go." Experiment until you find a form of words that feels most meaningful, so that you feel powerfully convinced. Overnight your intention, the actions you have taken and perhaps even a dream or two, will help the process of your release.

In the morning do you have more energy? Do you feel lighter and happier? Refreshed and renewed? If so, the process is working as it does best, to free up energies which are trapped in your past, so that more power is available to you to use now, when you need it.

The process of releasing old emotion trapped from the past is not always easy or straightforward; and progress often comes in fits and starts, as if to test our resolve. The amount of subconscious resistance we encounter reveals how deeply held our old beliefs are.

For example, I have been saying aloud, challenging the Universe to disagree with me, "I intend to be happy all day today!" This time last week I felt as if I was on a permanent holiday, smiling and laughing. Life moved forward smoothly and gracefully, amazingly well. Just imagine, I was saying to myself, if I could feel this good all the time. The realization that there was nothing to stop me made me feel even happier.

This week, the picture is slightly different. Two days ago I started to feel ill. I hurt my back, I ache all over and I got a head cold. My food intake is down and I have been eating lots of rubbish because I can't be bothered to cook. Funnily enough, I take it as a good sign: pain which has been locked in the body needs somewhere to go; and "good pain" can be very revealing.

I keep repeating, "I intend to be happy today!" and the location and intensity of the pain makes increasingly certain that this change is worth persisting with. Older patterns of resignation and defeatism lurking in my subconscious are finally loosening their grip. I am weathering a small storm on the way to a change in perspective. No doubt there will be others. I intend to keep going with this forgiveness thing, because the past is over and need not contaminate the present. I no longer wish to allow soiled, squint, memories of the past to overshadow my present. Now feels good.

LIVING IN THE PRESENT

With much justification, we often see our lives comprising what we did yesterday and what we will do at the weekend. While chuckling fondly over happy memories we make practical preparations to meet the future, for everything that is happening today, tomorrow or next week. I have to collect my daughter from school in two hours. We are going to visit Grandma on Friday. We fully expect these things to happen and chances are, they will. Yet it is a pity that so much of the time we live this way: we recall with great pleasure the wonderful chat we had with our friends at the club last weekend and look forward to seeing them again; we book our summer holidays in January; I just have to get through Friday and then I can enjoy a fabulous weekend off; I just have to reach retirement and then I can spend the money I have been saving all these years.

Time gives us precious opportunities to refine our choices. As time moves us forward, we can become clearer about what we choose and discover what makes us happiest. Most of us choose to be happy and I do believe that the happier we are, the closer we come to running the kind of race we came here to run.

Perhaps happiness is elusive because we have become accustomed to living as if yesterday and tomorrow are all that count: how can we be happy yesterday or next week? Don't we often say, "I plan to do this, enjoy myself, finally have a holiday *when...*"? The problem with tying our lives together with the tape of memories and spicing them up with the thrill of the future is that the thrill of being here NOW has a habit of evaporating altogether.

Memories have only a passing reality. Certainly there are photographs around our homes, but that picture of a beloved nephew on my bookshelf is a representation from the past. My own body has recreated itself, in its entirety, something like eight times since I was born. There is not one part of me which was with me when I first appeared to the outside world.

Tomorrow is even less certain: we don't have memories of the future lying around to remind us of where we will be going or what we will be doing in April next year. Yet we ponder the future constantly, perhaps holding fast to a hope that our future is bound to be better than now. But when do we ever arrive in the future?

As a daily exercise – especially when it doesn't feel true – I find it useful to remind myself that the only tool I really have at my disposal is my time and not even my yesterdays or my tomorrows, but my time now *in the present*. I easily forget that the only thrill which actually means anything is the one I am experiencing now. Deliberately slowing my pace so that I become more aware of this, I automatically feel happier and more relaxed: if now is all I have, what is there to worry about? Not a lot. One second at a time? I believe I could handle that.

Living *now* makes each pulsing moment electric, vivid and colourful, much more exciting than a lukewarm re-hash of something I did back then. Fundamentally, the present is all we have. Everything else is a "has been" or a "might be". Fully dwelling in the present allows our days to stretch wide, empty of thoughts over what is past and done with or worries about what might happen in the future. Now, using this understanding, we can fill our days with thoughts about what makes us feel good at this moment. Now feels easy to be around.

Similarly, we seem to love to *doing* lots of stuff, do we not? We wash dishes and clothes, we shop and rush from pillar to post, from our work to our homes and back. We make stuff and do things all the time. Of course we do and it is very difficult to see that we have much choice – we have to eat, sleep and work.

Even so, how many of us make a virtue of our preoccupations so that we are not left alone in the stillness? We fill whole days with thinking and doing, rather than being still, which ensures that we have no time to reflect. And, curiously unable to prioritize our peace of mind and our enjoyment, we will do anything – water the plants, polish shoes, go shopping, phone friends, spend hours on the internet – rather than make progress with what lies nearest our heart's desire. By the time our lists are all ticked and finished and we grind to a halt, we are very likely to slouch tiredly on the couch or fall asleep. A state of constant exhaustion is an ideal way to avoid being alone.

But it's time to face the truth: the bulk of daily tasks we set out to accomplish in our "determined" frame of mind are very often as appealing as cold soup. We manage them by rote, thoughtlessly clouding our horizons with worry and needless stress. I understand that. So instead of sliding about in an anaemic swill of anxiety about the jobs we "should" be doing, I would like to suggest a better way. Let it alone. Sit still for ten minutes after supper. Walk away from all the things you "should" do or the people you "need to" get in touch with. If it helps, take off your watch or your shoes as a gesture to free yourself from this time-bound mentality and give yourself permission to leave all that "stuff" alone for now.

I have a new saying which I fall back on gratefully, any time I feel that I am doing too much or going about life in the wrong spirit: *There is nothing I need to do.* Most of my friends think me eccentric and laugh as they pass me in a hurry on the way to their next job. However, for me this understanding clarifies that life works best when I let it carry me along peacefully. I cannot push time along or force life to work better for me by worrying, though I certainly make it more difficult. In a calmer, more trusting frame of mind, everything feels lighter and easier. And since there is nothing I *have* to do, my tasks lose their usual air of drudgery.

Being, allows refreshing honesty into our lives. We can be sad, we can be tired or dwell peacefully among the things we enjoy or let our minds wander. In choosing to be, every moment that we live totally in the present becomes supercharged, vivid and colourfully intense. Like electricity, each pulsing second moves us; the peace and strength in present silence can be as potent as ropes of silver or songs of golden light spinning circles of delicious possibility. All of this is revealed for us when we stop dodging the strength in Now and live embraced within its power.

In growing more comfortable with a state of being, we have more space to attend to anything that makes us feel bad, sad or uncomfortable. To discover what I don't like, all I have to do is do nothing. By listening to the silence I finally discover what I enjoy, what I desire and what would make me happy now. Being releases our genuine feelings, so that they swim to the surface of our lives and say hello – at last.

It really is that easy to re-direct our precious energy to the things which make us feel good and on a very practical level, to discover what we would enjoy doing next. We do not have to chase after, pursue or try to hold onto anything. Simply being means we have finally arrived. Therefore, being content in the present is restful.

You don't have to take my word for it. I like to think that, in the series *Conversations with God,* no less an authority than divinity suggests: (15) "When you come *from* "happiness", you do certain things because you *are* happy – as opposed to the old paradigm in which you did things that you hoped would make you happy...Whether you are trying to "be" happy, "be" wise, "be" love – you cannot "get there" by doing...*There is nothing you have to do.* You want to be happy? *Be happy.* You want to be wise? *Be wise.* You want to be love? *Be love.*"

The next time you are tempted to fill your morning with worthy tasks – but you honestly feel you would rather not – remind yourself that you do not need to do anything. For now, just be. That admission very quickly sets you free.

UNCONDITIONAL LOVE

"'What would love do now?" No other question is relevant, no other question is meaningful, no other question has any importance to your soul." (16)

Learning to love unconditionally is perhaps the greatest secret of happiness and our greatest challenge. This single idea presents us with real opportunities for growth and maturing, though if you think unconditional love is for sweet-natured angels, think again. Do you think unconditional love is easy? I don't. Perhaps I know a little about what it means intellectually, but finding ways to express it challenges me every day.

I struggle daily with forgiveness, with letting go of the small offences that pile around me and with suspending my judgment of different situations. Even so, somehow I am inching forward, increasingly aware that beyond this next summit of forgiveness lies a new horizon where we rediscover the freedom to love without setting *any* conditions.

We find *conditional* love easier to understand. When I am thoughtless I fall back into it often. This kind of "love" brings with it sharp expectations that YOU should do what I EXPECT, BEFORE I can love you. Conditional love shifts the blame for anything less than perfect onto that person whom we consider falls short in our estimation. We all know that conditions around this type of love lurk everywhere. We easily recognise them in thoughts such as, "(I love you if you) get good grades at school" or "(I approve of you, as long as you) do not disappoint me" or perhaps, "You are not the man I thought you were." Expectations such as these limit the giving and receiving of affection to times when we feel it is appropriate, deserving or has been earned.

Our offerings of affection and care usually bring hopes and expectations with them; and in the name of love, we all say and do things that we later regret. Yet recognizing how often I expect others to please me reveals how my love for them is tied in with burdensome conditions. My love has become unconvincing.

There is a saying that love is blind. True Love remains steady, whatever external conditions it encounters, encompassing all manner of persons and situations, regardless of appearances or apparent differences that allow less-than-perfect love to intrude. Unconditional love, which is the only real love, cannot be contained. It is the love that gives each one of us total permission to respect and be completely ourselves. Armed with our awareness of this freedom, we at last stand tall, released from the chains we wrap around ourselves. In the same spirit, we aim to cherish all others so that their lights shine brightly. There is no shadow of judgment to cloud that brightness.

It may be our experience that love is difficult and that love hurts. Love which sees and accepts totally, without setting conditions, is often painful. As we notice apparent unfairness, suffering and injustice, we may judge these conditions and call them "bad" or "unfair". Even so, true love sees us as we are and accepts our current place without judgment. Unconditional love waits in the wings to be rediscovered wherever we are, whether we are sorry, sad, in pain or suffering. It has never gone away from us, though it remains obscured because we have come to believe that "real" life is demanding and complicated.

Maybe your son just broke a window in your greenhouse, the third pane of glass he has smashed this month. Isn't it a good thing that your son is playing outside? When closely examined, you may grudgingly admit your "greenhouse", a dangerous pile of glass and rubble, is one of your quasi-athletic attempts to feel better, in spite of your lack of enthusiasm. Another broken pane of glass may be just the push you need to take yourself outside where you notice what a beautiful day it is and see that your wisteria is finally flowering. You hear the birds singing and as you are standing there, you reflect that perhaps it is time your greenhouse was demolished and the garden tidied up. So, after all, your son did you a favour.

Most situations which we might call "annoying" actually contain a germn of something positive, which it is easier to see when we smile and relax instead of frowning. Love is not all about grand gestures, expensive vacations and posh hotels. Looking in someone's eyes for the truth goes straight to the heart of what matters.

Unconditional love does not ask us to accept constant bad behaviour; nor are we expected to be total martyrs. If my daughter misbehaves, it is unloving of me to condone this in her all the time. I know she needs me to set limits, to show her what she can do and what is not allowed in our household. It is my job as her parent to be unpopular, to sometimes say "No" and stick to my guns when I choose to. But in our battle of wills I do occasionally relent, because it would be unloving of me to be too rigid; and there is never any suggestion that I withhold love or make her good behaviour a condition of my love for her.

Loving unconditionally requires us, among other things, to acknowledge that Life does not need our judgments or our aggression for its defence. We may stand around the perimeter fence at Fort Worth Naval Air Station and argue with the soldiers inside the wire, but if we are rude to them or if we throw rocks at them, our behaviour is fuelling mutual hostility and dislike.

If you have followed this book through to this point, I hope that finally accepting the value of love without conditions comes quite easily. If not and if you still feel there is something missing in your life, I invite you to affirm, "I am worthy, *therefore* I surround myself with kind friends. I take plenty of rest. I am kind to myself..." until your remaining resistance and disbelief melt away. We are all imperfect, yet in the sight of Life, our imperfections make us perfect. What is more, we cannot resist the inevitable truth dawning, that we each of us deserve to enjoy happiness, in whatever way we may achieve it and however it comes to us.

Learning to love ourselves unconditionally is a very powerful, permanent way to find peace with ourselves and others, to live calmly with all the contradictions we unearth every day. Finally, the old law, "Do unto others as you would have them do to you," bears fruit in the here and now and for always.

THE JOURNEY HOME

It is some months since I completed the "final" version of this text. For me, one of the slowest learners on the planet, happiness is at last beginning to come together and blossom as part of my everyday reality. I forgive and let go more easily and feel happier. I smile when I make mistakes. My cell memories are changing as I allow happiness in, though at times progress is frustratingly slow. However, after thirty years looking at life through distorted lenses, I can cut myself a little slack. My small beginnings are taking their sweet time to grow, but I like to think that they are being well planted and nourished with optimism and growing patience.

Whoever we are, whether we are limping, sick, sad, disillusioned or sore; whether we are bitter, guilt-ridden, unfulfilled or dying, we are always included in life, light and love. Whether we see it or not, we can, whatever our condition, make a choice to be loving, happy, joyful.

With every breath we take, we choose what we

desire and more clearly define who we are. Every pulse in time gives us a choice for this way or that, this thought or that one. Every option is there, every possibility is before us. To reclaim the best for ourselves, is to re-connect with the feelings we each had, before expectation and disappointment took hold. In the long ago days, before our happiness was driven out of us, we knew what made our eyes sparkle. We each knew what we desired and enjoyed. We each of us chose spontaneity and we can *choose it again now.*

NOTES

1) Thomas Hobbes – *Leviathan,* Part 1, Chapter 13

2) Henry David Thoreau – "most men lead lives of quiet desperation and go to the grave with the song still in them." – *Civil Disobedience and Other Essays.*

3) Doreen Virtue – *The Lightworkers' Way,* page 196

4) Lynn Grabhorn – *Excuse Me, Your Life Is Waiting: The Astonishing Power of Positive Feelings*

5) Louise Hay – *You Can Heal Your Life*

6) David Wells – *Past, Present And Future: What Your Past Lives Tell You About yourself*

7) *"Je pense, donc je suis"* – Rene Descartes – *Discourse on the Method (1637);* also *"Cogito, ergo sum"* appears in *Principles of Philosophy (1644)*

8) *Collins English Dictionary*, HarperCollins publishers, updated 3rd Edition

9) Kahlil Gibran – *The Prophet,* page 61

10) Foundation For Inner Peace – *A Course in Miracles* page 378

11) Foundation For Inner Peace – *A Course in Miracles* page 330

12) Ekhart Tolle – *The Power of Now*

13) Neale Donald Walsch – *Conversations With God* Volume 1, page 101

14) Louise L Hay, *You Can Heal Your Life* Hay House, 2007 edition

15) Neale Donald Walsch – *Conversations With God* Volume 3 page 363

16) Neale Donald Walsch – *Conversations With God* Volume 1, p 130

APPENDIX

Prayer of St Francis of Assisi

Lord, make Me an Instrument of Thy Peace

Where there is hatred, let me sow Love

Where there is injury, Pardon;

Where there is doubt, Faith;

Where there is despair, Hope;

Where there is darkness, Light;

Where there is sadness, Joy.

O Divine Master, Grant that I may seek

Not so much to be consoled as to console;

To be understood as to understand;

To be loved as to love;

For it is in giving that we receive;

It is in pardoning that we are pardoned;

And it is in dying

That we are born to Eternal Life

Amen

SOURCES AND SUGGESTIONS FOR FURTHER READING

Deepak Chopra, *The Book of Secrets*, Harmony Books, 2004 and *Quantum Healing* Bantam Books, 1989, 1990

Dr. Henry Cloud, & Dr. John Townsend, *Boundaries – When to say Yes, When to say No to Take Control of Your Life*, USA, Zondervan, 1992.

Diana Cooper, *A Little Light on the Spiritual Laws* Hodder & Stoughton, 2004

Betty Eadie, *Embraced by the Light* Harper Element 1992

Gill Edwards, *Living Magically,* Piatkus, 1991

Foundation for Inner Peace, *A Course in Miracles* 1996

The Book of Christian Discipline of the Yearly Meeting of the Religious Society of Friends (Quakers) in Britain. 1995, 2005

Kahlil Gibran, *The Prophet* Heinemann, 1972

Lynn Grabhorn, *Excuse Me, your Life is Waiting: The Astonishing Power of Positive Feelings,* Hodder & Stoughton, 2004

Trutz Hardo, *Children Who Have Lived Before,* Verlag die Silberschnur, 2000

Louise L Hay, *You Can Heal Your Life* Hay House, 2007 edition

Michael Henderson, *Forgiveness: Breaking the Chain of Hate,* Grosvenor Books, 2002

Esther and Jerry Hicks, *Ask and it is given: The Teachings of Abraham,* Hay House, 2005

Anne Jones, *Heal Yourself,* Piatkus, 2002

Elizabeth Kubler-Ross, *On Life After Death,* Celestial Arts, 1991

Mark Kurlansky, *Non Violence – The History of a Dangerous Idea,* Jonathan Cape, 2006

Paul Lambillion, *Auras and Colours* ,Gateway, Gill & Macmillan Ltd 2001

William McDonough, & Michael Braungart, *Cradle to Cradle – Remaking the Way We Make Things,* North Point Press, 2002

Jim Pym, *Listening To the Light,* Rider Books, 1999

Estelle Roberts, *Fifty Years a Medium,* SDU Publications, 2006

Eckhart Tolle, *The Power of Now,* Hodder & Stoughton, 2001

Jason Vale, *Slim 4 Life: Freedom from the Food Trap,* Thorsons, 2002

Doreen Virtue, *The Lightworker's Way,* Hay House UK Ltd, 2005

David Wells, *Past, Present and Future: What your Past Lives Tell You about Yourself* Hay House UK Ltd, 2007

Brian Weiss, *Same Soul, Many Bodies,* Piatkus, 2004

Marie Woodall, *Secrets of a High Heeled Healer,* Thorson Element, an imprint of Harper Collins, 2003

Neale Donald Walsch, *Conversations with God, Books One, Two and Three* Hodder & Stoughton, 1995 et seq.

ABOUT FRAN MACILVEY

Fran was born in Congo in 1965 and spent eight years at boarding school in Scotland. She qualified in law and worked as a solicitor for ten years before turning to her first love, writing. Her memoir, *Trapped: My Life with Cerebral Palsy* (Skyhorse Publishing 2014 / 2016) is an Amazon international bestseller.

Happiness Matters and her third book *Making Miracles* explore how we can all find more happiness and fulfilment in life - what Fran calls, "gleaning something valuable from forty years of making mistakes." If you have enjoyed reading *Happiness Matters* please consider writing a review.

Fran is currently also writing a series of novels about women in the law. In her spare time she reads, swims, blogs, rides a lovely horse called Fudge, sings in the shower and dances where no-one can see her.

If you would like to contact Fran, please email franmacilvey@fastmail.fm or contact her at http://www.franmacilvey.com or through the Scottish Book Trust, of which she is a participating author.

Thank you to... literary consultant Claire Wingfield, Diane Dickson, Frank Kusy, Janet Hughes, Rebecca Hislop, Julie D'Amour, Chris Longmuir, The Alliance of Independent Authors, Elouise Renich Fraser, Dilek Taylor, Everyone at User 2 Computers, Bernie Leslie, Carol Graham, Catherine Lenderi, Cherry Gregory, Dana Goodman, David Price, Diana Noel-Paton and everyone at The Thistle Foundation, Doug Simpson, Emma Crees, Fleur Boyle, John Bayliss, John Phillips, Kerstin Phillips, Joy Godfrey, Judy Adams, Karen Concannon, Lucinda E Clarke, Margaret Skea, Majk Stokes, Patti Tingen, Ruth Needle, Steven Whitacre, Tom Breheny.

Lightning Source UK Ltd.
Milton Keynes UK
UKOW05f2216010617
302449UK00006B/23/P